THE CREATIVE CONVERSATION *ArtMaking as Playful Prayer*

Book Design: Gary Robbins
Edited by: Jill Kelly PhD.

Published by Eyes Aflame Publishing

Portland, OR

Address Permissions to:
Eyes Aflame Publishing
Permissions
PO Box 4076
Portland, OR 97208

Disclaimer: The author and publisher have made every attempt to insure that all instructions given in this book are accurate and safe, but the author and publisher expressly disclaim any and all liability, of whatever type, whether direct or consequential, and however arising from the use of this book. The techniques and advice in this book are not intended to diagnose or treat any illness or disease, nor should this book be used as a substitute for treatment of any illness or disease. The materials and techniques in this book are not intended for children.

Library of Congress Control Number: 2011941266
ISBN 978-0-9844568-0-2
Printed in Canada

The Creative Conversation

ArtMaking as Playful Prayer

Bridget Benton

TO DARREN, *You are my rock, my paper, my scissors, my lizard, and my Spock.*

TO LESLIE, *Who saw me as an artist even when I didn't.*

TO JILL, *Without whom this book might never have reached completion.*

Acknowledgements

No book is written in a vacuum; it's too dark and it sucks. So, I would like to thank the members of the beautiful un-vacuum-like creative community I have had the pleasure of working in:

- Dr. Jill Kelly, editor, writing coach, and deadly Quiddler player
- All the women of Writing Fridays and the Aldermarsh Retreats
- All the folks who bravely served as test readers and made this book better, including Leslie Peterson, Diane Archer, Jan Underwood, Annie Rousseau, Leah Piken Kolidas, Diane Gilleland, Deborah Hobbie, Gretchin Lair, and Janice Francisco
- My professors and fellow students at the International Center for Studies in Creativity at Buffalo State College campus of the State University of New York who first saw the potential of this work, including Dr. Mary Murdock and Dr. Cyndi Burnett
- Linda Womack and all the other wonderful folks in the Portland Chapter of the International Encaustic Artists
- The beautiful people of Scarlet Star Studios
- Jackie, Tammy, Yevette, Jo-el, Noah and all the folks at the PCC Small Business Development Center who know that business is creative
- Sister Diane and the whole creative blogging community
- Mark Silver at Heart of Business for his penetrating questions and Shams Cohen for recommending him
- Maria Raleigh at Collage, the art store that understands mixed-media artists
- Peter Rossing at Muse Art and Design for his ongoing support
- Jen Neitzel for working with me to offer so many teaching opportunities at DIY Lounge
- Stewart Cubley, fearless leader of the Painting Experience
- Helen McCann, for being a great friend, top-notch accountant, and the first person to take an Artmaking as Playful Prayer class
- Robyn Lee Williams, who was dubious about the whole prayer thing yet still came back for more and brought her friends
- And finally, every student who has ever put their creative trust in my hands and taken an art workshop from me

Table of Contents

Introduction
Where This Book Came from:
My Story

It was 2003, and his question made me cry.

I had recently quit a corporate job in market research, taken a long trip through Asia, and returned to the U.S. with no idea of what to do with my life. I had one failed art business under my belt already, and I was trying to figure out how to make a go of another one. So I had enlisted the services of a business consultant with a spiritual focus.

We were sitting on the patio of a local restaurant. The sun was glaring, the picnic bench was hard, and I was uncomfortable. We were talking about my business. I wanted to bring my spirituality into my work with other people, and I wanted to be creative, and I wanted to help other people be more spiritual and creative.

"So what is your regular spiritual practice?" he asked.

And I started crying because I knew I didn't really have one.

I had been raised Presbyterian, discovered the joy of the Divine Feminine in college, then worked the 12 Steps and engaged wholeheartedly in Wiccan ritual celebration of the seasons as a young adult. In my late 20s and early 30s, I worked extensively with a Shamanic healer, visited peaceful Buddhist temples, reveled in the beauty of Hindu art, and enjoyed enlightening conversations with my Sufi friends.

God grant me serenity to accept the things I cannot change, courage to change the things I can, and wisdom to know the difference.

–Reinhold Niebuhr

In each of these explorations, I had experienced moments of deep peace, joy, connectedness, energy, focus, and inspiration that I identified as the presence of the Divine. I had even briefer moments of feeling cleansed, like my ego had dropped away and been replaced with an overwhelming awareness of how I was an insignificant yet essential part of something so much larger. These experiences had led me to acknowledge and embrace a Divine presence that was both a part of me and greater than everything I knew. Yet none of the practices I had explored had become a regular part of my life.

With that one question, I felt this business consultant had just seen through me and labeled me a big, phony New-Age flake. It didn't help that my current boyfriend, an evangelical Christian, had recently challenged me for my lack of spiritual focus. Crying just seemed like the appropriate response.

I don't remember much about the rest of that conversation though I do remember the consultant talking about his own spiritual practice and how it had evolved. Finally, the clouds of my self-judgment cleared, and over the next weeks and months I began to think about what a spiritual practice really was. And what it wasn't.

It wasn't about being born into and following a particular faith, and it wasn't just about engaging in the rituals of a faith either.

A spiritual practice, as I began to understand it, was a discipline. It was a discipline in the do-something-consistently-and-stick-to-it-in-order-to-learn-something way rather than the meditate-for-an-hour-a-day-no-matter-what way. After all, I realized, you learn things by practicing. I needed to do something on a consistent basis that would strengthen my spiritual muscles and help me stay in touch with Spirit. I needed to pick a path and walk it.

Now, consistent practice has never been my strong suit. Ask my friends and family about how I do with "staying in touch" and you will hear tales of long silences followed by bursts of intense, focused contact. This pattern is echoed in the way I have approached just about everything in my life—from housecleaning to homework.

Still, I began to look back at all the times that I had felt connected and deeply aware of Spirit. Hiking in the woods, drawing, taking photographs, teaching, nurturing beauty, painting, being in community, dancing, cooking, creating, writing, performing, connecting with friends: These were all things that helped me stay in touch with the presence of Spirit in my life. These were all things that had the potential to help me

build a relationship with Spirit. These creative, connective activities had the potential to be the basis of my spiritual practice; in fact, they had formed the essence of my spirituality all along.

Of course, the challenge was that I had some of the same issues with my art as I had with my spirituality: I lacked a regular practice, frequently felt disconnected and blocked, and simply wasn't going as deep as I knew I could.

As a little girl, I loved drawing and painting and making things. As I grew older, I was labeled as artistic, talented, and creative. I enjoyed—even craved—the approval, and I was also scared that I wouldn't be able to live up to the expectations those labels implied.

So guess what? The older I got, the harder it got to make art. The more I tried to make good art, the less joy there was in it. Yet I majored in art as an undergrad and made a business of batiked and silkscreened clothing fresh out of college. Even when I was doing corporate work or traveling, I was writing and taking pictures and trying to paint. I attempted Julia Cameron's *The Artist's Way* half a dozen times. Still, the joy remained largely elusive, as did the good art. Then, in 2000, I had a breakthrough of sorts: I took a process painting workshop with Stewart Cubley.

Stewart Cubley and Michele Cassou developed their painting workshops based on Michele's experiences painting with children. She saw a joy in their creative exploration that she, as an adult artist, had lost contact with. When I first stepped up to the table filled with bright tempera paints and decided which pot of color to dip my brush in, I was grinning. My brush dripping with magenta paint, I started painting a face. I painted a lot of faces. For five days, I made paintings with an energy and a focus I had forgotten I was capable of. I felt like a kid again.

I realized that as an artist, I knew very little about how creativity and the creative process worked. So I started reading. I studied other artists who had developed programs based on the joy of making and the healing power of art. I began to look away from art made for galleries and museums, and to look toward art made out of need, art made for meaning and personal expression. I took more workshops with Stewart Cubley and from other process-oriented artists. I became more and more interested in devotional art from different spiritual traditions. I quit my corporate job and traveled to Bali. There, art-making is such a part of life and spiritual practice that there is no word in their language for "art" or "artist," much as we do not have a separate word in English for "person who breathes."

Which brings me back to the hard picnic bench in the warm summer of 2003, sobbing in front of a man I barely knew. Even though I had rediscovered my joy in artmaking and was delighting in my nibbles at the spiritual buffet, I hadn't developed a true practice in either. Realizing how they were connected in my own life meant that I was taking my first real step on that path. It was time to get serious. It was time to get walking.

A year later, I invited some friends to participate in the first Artmaking as Playful Prayer group. Teaching and sharing the techniques and discoveries helped me to understand what I was doing in a deeper way. Going back to school in 2005 to get a Master's of Science in Creative Studies (rather than the Master's of Fine Arts degree everyone expected) helped me to understand the theories behind my practice and helped me learn to apply my practice more consistently.

This book has come out of my own work, my research, the classes I have taken, the classes I have taught, and my on-going efforts to develop a true practice. It is both an attempt to synthesize all the creativity books I have ever read and to share the unique things I have learned and experienced.

I don't claim to have all the answers. I'm still learning and figuring things out. This book represents one more step in my practice. It is one more way to deepen my understanding of what I'm doing and to continue giving back what I've learned. And

it's likely that you won't agree with everything you read here. That's good. See where challenging my notions takes you.

My hope is that this book will help you find a way to more fully engage with your own creativity in a meaningful way. Doing my own work, the most important things I have learned are to be conscious of my intentions, to regularly do the work of artmaking, to make with a focus on process rather than product, to reach out and connect with others, and finally, to listen deeply to my own inner voice. These simple actions are the basis of my practice, and what I hope to share with you.

Chapter 1
Making This Book Your Own

Who Can Use This Book

- You can be scared of artmaking and use this book.
- You can feel incapable of drawing a straight line and use this book.
- You can feel creatively blocked and use this book.
- You can be uncomfortable with the idea of prayer and use this book.
- You can be painting every day and use this book.
- You can be an art teacher and use this book.
- You can doubt the existence of God and use this book.
- You can be getting ready for a big gallery show and use this book.
- You can be a Christian, a Buddhist, or a Sufi and use this book.
- You can be a writer, an engineer, an addict, a mother, or a dancer and use this book.

If you have an interest in creativity and spirituality, you can use this book. You don't have to have even a single minute of experience making art although it may help if you have always secretly wanted to be an artist or are the kind of person who notices the way light glints off the surface of the ocean, gazes longingly at displays of oil pastels, or has dreamed of finger painting. You may be at a crossroads or in a place of transition. You may find that you are looking for a way into making art more regularly or with more passion or that you are looking to bring a little more meaning into your everyday life.

All that is required is a longing for a richer creative life and greater connection. It is these things that will help you make this book your own.

What This Book Offers

This book offers up ideas and exercises to get you working with creativity—and artmaking specifically—as a process that supports your spiritual journey. I break this process of creativity down into five components:

Getting Clear: Intention
Getting Inspired: Energy
Getting Engaged: Action
Staying in Touch: Intuition
Giving Back: Community

In the Artmaking as Playful Prayer workshops, students discover this process through a series of artmaking exercises, group discussions, and individual projects. In this book, I lay out the process explicitly as well as providing you with opportunities for hands-on exploration.

I have found that working with this process, and the 12 key attitudes and actions that support the work of artmaking, has helped my students relax and enjoy their artmaking more. It has also helped them take a more spiritual and intuitive approach to their artmaking.

How to Use This Book

There is no right or wrong way to use this book. Each person will come to this book from a different place. So I designed it as a home companion, a guide to help you engage your creativity more fully. Like any true friend, it is designed to meet you where you are.

The Introduction and Chapter 1 are welcoming, getting-to-know-you chapters. Chapter 1 (yes, this chapter!) also offers up the first of many hands-on Artful Explorations that get you exploring the attitudes and actions that support your Artmaking asPlayful Prayer practice. Materials are listed for each Exploration. I try to keep the materials simple or, when they're not, offer a simpler version of the project as an option. You may find that you already have much of what you need. (If not, you can skip to the Basic Materials section in Chapter 4 for a quick shopping list.)

Chapter 2 gives you an overview of the main ideas covered in more depth later in the book as well as asking you to consider your own ideas. Chapter 3 is an introduction to making space for making art and includes the first of many Conversations. These Conversations are opportunities to journal, ask yourself some probing questions, and do a little self-discovery. Chapter 4 reviews all of the materials needed for the Explorations and Conversations in the book and supports you in choosing materials to work with.

Chapters 5 through 11 are the core of the program, challenging you to think about and make art in different ways, supporting you through blocks, and helping you develop your artmaking as a regular spiritual practice and your creativity as a way of living. Each of these chapters includes at least one Conversation and two Artful Explorations, along with other opportunities to get your hands on the creative process. Chapter 12 is the pep talk, the warm hug, and the promise to stay in touch before we part.

Looking for Structure or Delicious Chaos?

If you are looking for structure and a guided approach to developing your creativity, you can follow the full 12-week home workshop program outlined in the Table of Contents, reading the Chapters and doing some of the Artful Explorations each week.

If you are feeling the need to bust out and shake things up in your creative life, you've probably already been skipping around and trying things out. Any way you choose to do it is just fine. How you choose to use the book will depend on what you most need, and I absolutely trust you to take care of yourself.

Mess It Up and Make It Your Own!

Whether you are craving structure or feeling the need to meander, and whether you have the paperback version or the digital version, I'd like to encourage you to mess this book up. You'll notice that many of the illustrations are simply begging to be doodled around or collaged over or used as the base for colorful over-painting. Some of the Artful Explorations will even ask you to mark in the book.

If you have the paperback version, please draw and color and paste in this book! If you have the digital version, please print it out and cut it up and paste it down and color over it! Make this book your own in the most visceral, tactile, concrete ways you can.

Just as you'll be making the book your own, I encourage you to make the art your own. I offer up ideas for Artful Explorations and I ask that you think of them as starting points. If you think of something you like better, do it. If you want to use different materials, do it. I offer tips and techniques, and I also know that you may find a way to do things that suits you better.

I try to keep the materials lists and the instructions for the projects fairly simple, which means they are ripe for intuition, exploration, and adaptation. Since these projects are process-oriented rather than product-oriented, your finished project will probably not look like any of the samples in the book—and that's good! It will look instead like something that you made, something that came from your heart and hands.

A Note to Members of Organized Faith Traditions

I believe that most of these projects are compatible with most faith traditions. If your faith restricts the construction of altars or the creation of representational art, feel free to be creative and adapt the projects as needed. I have attempted to offer a variety of alternatives so that each person can find if not the perfect project, at least a great starting point.

A Note to Professional Creatives and Caregivers

People who create for a living may benefit from the book in a different way. Finding or rediscovering spiritual meaning in your work can make the work richer and more satisfying. Taking an intuitive and process-oriented approach to your artwork can help you push through blocks and inspire new directions in your work. If you teach art, you may find new ideas for engaging your students. Similarly, if your primary job is to guide and care for the spirit of others, you may find that artmaking helps you ground and connect, and that you may have new ideas for engaging others in a creative and spiritual life.

An Introduction to Exploration

With the focus of our Western culture so firmly set on productivity, it can feel self-indulgent to take a quiet span to examine images of birds or look deeply at the colors in a sunset. It can feel like a waste of time to take a walk and pick up pretty rocks or cut images we like out of magazines.

Definition

Explore *verb:* To journey for the purpose of discovery rather than arrival. To investigate the unknown. To wander and gather information in unmapped places, deeply noticing, learning and daring dragons.

In fact, many of the activities labeled as Conversations or Artful Explorations in this book may seem like an extravagant expenditure of time. In them, we are invited to explore, to traverse creative ground for the sake of discovery, not destination. While these creative activities may not have predictable productive outcomes or impact our bottom line, they will impact our spirit.

Exploring is a simple way of being present, of being in the moment, of being mindful. It is an act of deepening our awareness and really looking. Exploration is about moving across uncharted territory, learning unexpected things as we go. These Artful Explorations are adventures. Even if you think you know the terrain, give yourself a chance to approach it from an explorer's perspective. Look deeply, notice details, and treat the path as though you have never walked it before.

You may not always be pleased with the results of these Explorations. I suggest you hang on to them anyway. Keep them in a folder, folio, or box. Going back and looking at them later, you may be surprised by the beauty they reveal or the value they hold for you. And you may discover that they can serve as the basis for a new project!

Like most people, I struggle quite regularly with placing value on the work I do as an artist and taking the time to do that work—including exploring. Sometimes it just feels easier to do the laundry. My advice is this: If you do decide to do the laundry, take the time to notice the colors and the textures. Make even that act an act of exploration.

Cardboard Camera

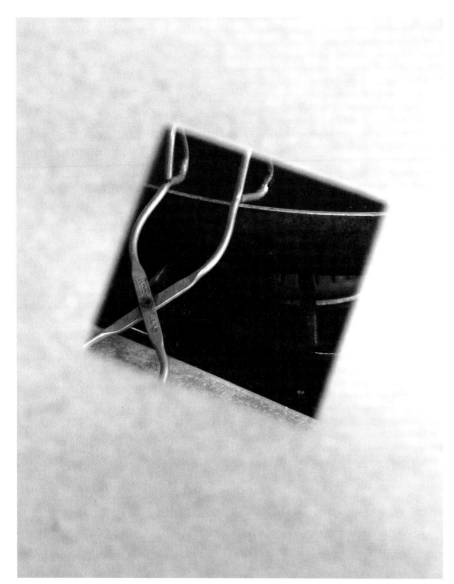

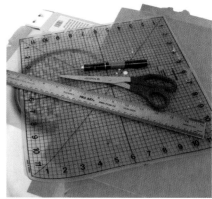

Materials

- Blank cardboard or stiff paper
- Scissors or craft knife
- Your eyes

OPTIONAL

- Straight edge or ruler (optional)
- Pen or pencil (optional)
- Cutting mat (optional)

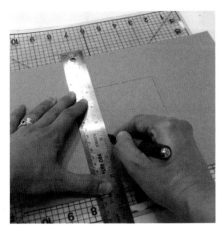

1. Take a piece of heavy paper or light cardboard that's 8"× 10" or larger and has a blank side. I've found that using one panel from an old cereal box works well. Cut a square—about 2" × 2"—out of the middle using scissors or a craft knife. Flip the cardboard so that the blank side is facing you.

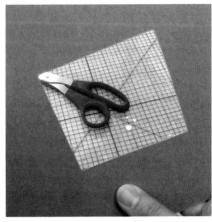

2. Now, hold the cardboard up and use it to frame part of what you can see and block off the rest. Move it around. Move yourself around, using what's interesting in the square to guide your movement. Move your arm away from your body and back in to "zoom in" and "zoom out" of the picture. Take the time to really notice the space around you, taking imaginary "snapshots." Try doing this in a space that you feel really familiar with and use it to explore the space and see it in new ways.

TAKING IT FURTHER

Additional Materials
- Real camera
- Sketch paper
- Pen or pencil

A. Take a camera (a camera phone will do fine) with you on a route you follow every day—the bedroom to the kitchen, your house to work, the kids' school to the gym—and try to see it like a tourist. Really notice it. Take pictures from new perspectives and capture the objects that you usually ignore.

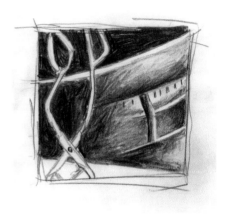

B. Experiment with taking your cardboard and a sketchbook to a mundane location you often visit—the grocery store, the gym, your own backyard. Frame shots with your cardboard and then sketch them out in your sketchbook using just a pen or pencil. Try getting really close or framing the objects so that they are not immediately recognizable. Close up, the objects turn into abstract compositions. This makes them much easier—and more fun—to draw!

Discard Collage

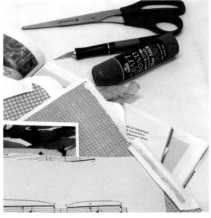

Materials
- Junk mail or old magazines
- Glue stick
- Scissors or craft knife
- Blank paper or sketchbook

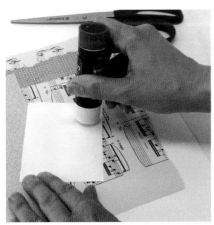 

1. Go through your junk mail for the day, the contents of your recycle bin, or a stack of magazines you're ready to give away or recycle. Give yourself no more than 15 minutes to explore these materials, keeping your eyes open for things that are visually interesting to you or things that grab you—words, pictures, patterns, textures, colors—and rip them out. Don't analyze your decisions: Just rip the images out and set them aside in a stack.

2. At the end of your 15 minutes, take a pair of scissors and a glue stick and begin to make a collage. Limit yourself to using only those things that you pulled out during your 15-minute session. You may be surprised by the patterns that emerge.

COLLAGE TIP: A glue stick is probably the easiest glue to use for collage. Just apply the glue to the back of your image and press it down where you want it! If you want to apply glue right up to the edge, try placing the image face down on some scrap paper or an old phone book so that any excess glue ends up on the scrap paper, not on your table or your collage!

Additional Materials
- Container for collected collage materials
- Pen or pencil

A. Spend a few minutes every day sorting through your junk mail, catalogs, old magazines or greeting cards and tossing those items with potential into a box for future collage use. You'll be amazed at how quickly you build up a supply of interesting collage images.

B. After you've finished a collage, take a few moments to write about the piece, either on the back of the collage or in a journal. You might consider writing about how it felt to make the piece, the patterns that emerged in the images you selected, or what you learned from doing the piece.

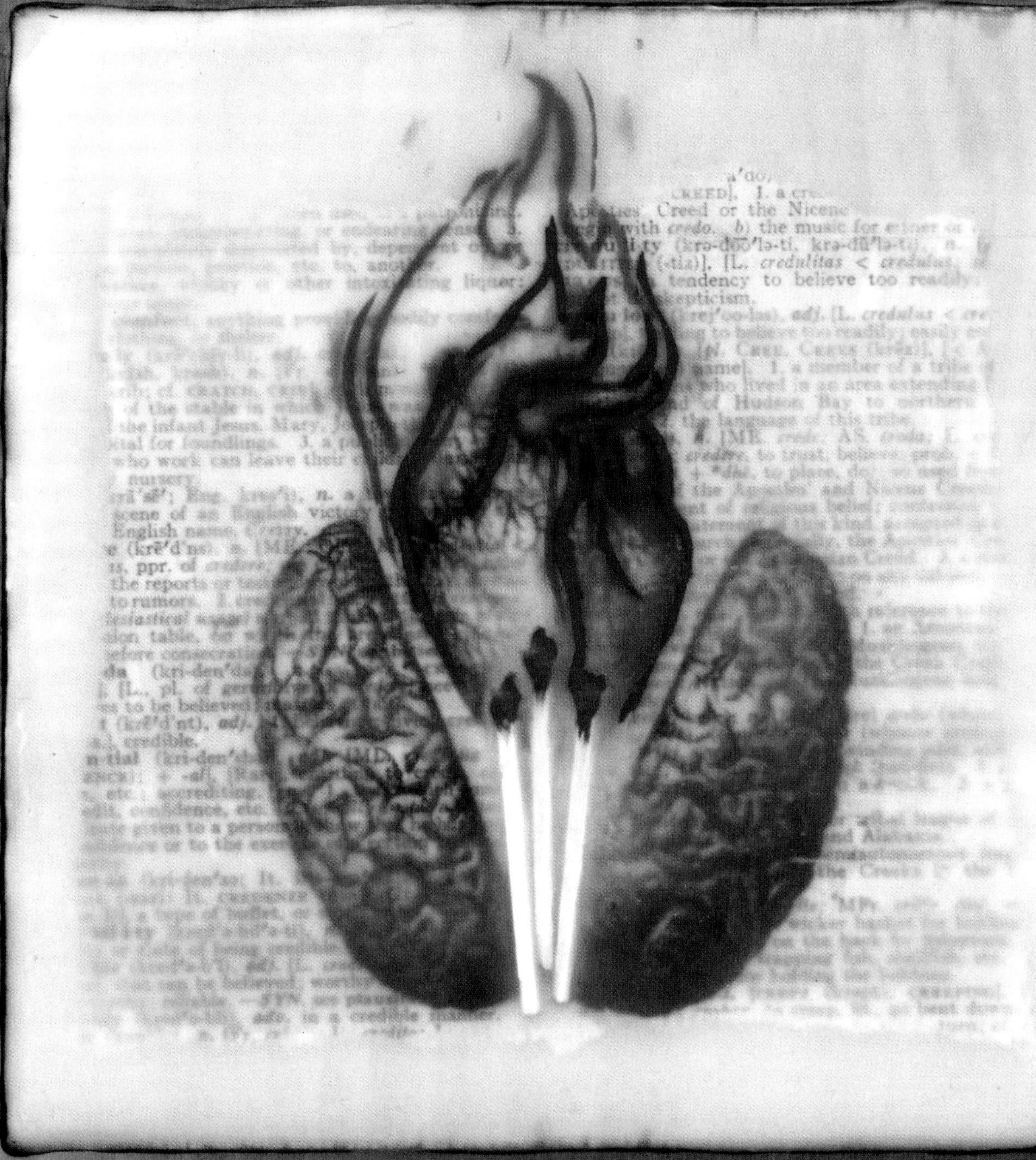

Chapter 2
What Is ArtMaking
as Playful Prayer?

Defining Terms

Artmaking as playful prayer is making art as a spiritual practice.

And it's a lot more. It's a way of making art that is freeing and intuitive and playful. It's a way of connecting with Spirit that is at once dynamic and meditative. It is a way of deeply listening and deeply noticing. It's an attitude, a process, and a practice.

Artmaking as playful prayer is a creative conversation.

Artmaking as playful prayer isn't a monolog; it's a conversation between you and the art, a conversation between you and an energy that pulses through everything. Then, there are those amazing moments when the conversation drops away, the sense of separateness drops away, and you and the art and the universe all become one. In those moments, it can feel as though you have become a channel for the flow of that universal energy.

For me, artmaking is how I move from the monolog of my own ego and emotions to the conversation and ultimately to the channel. And channeling that flow is a deeply spiritual experience for me. A friend and I were recently joking that a good day in the studio was working for four hours and having 40 seconds of flow. To make art as part of a spiritual practice, we have to learn how to get out of the way.

What We Bring with Us

Chances are that if you've picked up this book, you already feel that link between your creativity and your spirituality. You probably recognize yourself as a creative and a spiritual being. You've probably had moments of experiencing that flow, perhaps while making art, perhaps while doing something else.

The position of the artist is humble. He is essentially a channel.

–Piet Mondrian

You may also exist, as I do, in a culture that has a lot of *baggage* around both art and spirituality. Culturally, words like *artist* or *playful* carry associations that we're not consciously aware of but that can still affect us. You may feel like you can't be an artist, or you may feel blocked. Sometimes a shift in how we think about words like *art* can open up whole new realms of possibility.

Recently, I was teaching an evening class that was heavy on new techniques involving wax and fiber. The class was tired, I hadn't brought enough wax, and the students were feeling frustrated. During a break, I presented the idea of artmaking as a conversation they could have rather than a product they had to control, and there were several sharp intakes of breath, some widening eyes, and a few exclamations of "Oh!" This was immediately followed by the sound of people digging back into their projects with renewed fervor. Acknowledging that they didn't have to be in control was liberating for some of the students. Instead, they could respond to what was happening within the artwork itself.

What Is Art?

To get started, take a moment to consider your own definition of art. What do you usually think of when someone says the word *art*? Is it something beautiful or aesthetically pleasing? Something that hangs on a wall or sits in a gallery? Is it something that only certain people do? Is it something that you need special training to understand?

I know that for a long time I thought of art only as a finished object, and, as I mentioned earlier, I had the idea that the object had to be *good* to be *art*. Of course, I really didn't know what *good art* was, so that meant someone else had to judge it. Without consciously realizing it, every time I sat down to make art, I thought it had to be good and I had this sense that someone was waiting to judge me. As a result, I spent a lot more time worrying about making good art than I did actually making art.

When I first read Eric Booth's *The Everyday Work of Art* and he defined art as a verb, not a noun, I was blown away. His definition returned to the root origins of the word and uncovered the idea of art as "making something with meaning." This simple shift shook up my whole understanding of what art was. I began to understand that art could be an action and a process, not just a product. I began to understand art as more than what hangs on the gallery wall.

If art is really about intention and meaning, it means that a shawl woven with thoughts of care and protection can be art. An arrangement of photos and mementos to honor a relative can be art. A garden tended, a shelf built, a child nurtured, a story told: All of these have the potential to be art, as all of these have the potential to be the tangible record of a meaningful, mindful creative process.

If the process of making is mindful, the result can be art. If the object or action holds *meaning beyond its own self*, it can be art. Looking at art this way, *good* has nothing to do with it.

For me, art has become about how I approach the process—and about the process itself. And so I came up with my own definition of art, both as a verb and a noun, and I share that definition with you at the edge of the page. All of the definitions you'll see in this book are my own adaptations. While they owe much to online sources like Dictionary.com and print sources like the *Webster Unabridged Dictionary* and the *Word Origins Dictionary* that are mentioned in the resources section, I have added my own perspective and flourishes to each.

I have attempted to shift the cultural baggage loaded in each of these words so that the focus is on the meanings that are most relevant in the context of artmaking as playful prayer. I have included them here so that you will know what I mean when I use a given term—and as a launching point for your own reconsideration of these terms.

By using the term *artmaking*, I'm emphasizing art-as-verb. I'm focusing on the actions and attitudes that support artmaking as playful prayer. These actions and attitudes are also what I think of as the work of artmaking. All of these attitudes and actions are touched on throughout the book. There are also Conversations and Artful Explorations to help you try these different attitudes and actions on for size. Look over the list of 12 key actions and attitudes listed on the next page. Right now, they may not mean much. By the end of the book, however, I'm hoping that at least a few of them will be on their way to becoming artmaking habits.

Definition

Art *Verb:* To make something with meaningful, mindful intent (adapted from *The Everyday Work of Art*).
Noun: An action or process we are all capable of that serves as evidence of our own Divine spark; the tangible record of meaningful, mindful creative process.

Good art is not what it looks like, but what it does to us.

–Roy Adzak

The least of things with meaning is worth more in life than the greatest of things without it.

–Carl Jung

12 Attitudes and Actions of Artmaking as Playful Prayer

Explore
Focus on Process, Not Product
Defer Judgment
Be Like a Novice
Be in Conversation
Be Mindful
Follow the Energy
Let Go of the Outcome
Be Curious
Tune Up Your Inner Ears
Cultivate Appreciation and Gratitude
Hold Clear Intentions

My own work—and therefore the guidance and explorations in this book—are focused on visual art and craft. Yet the principles, actions, and attitudes apply to any creative endeavor: You can do the work of art as a writer, as a dancer, as a musician, as a teacher. To paraphrase Eric Booth, you can do the work of art in your everyday life.

What Is an Artist?

So, if we expand our definition of what art is, what happens to our idea of the artist? Consider your own definition, the ideas you had before you started reading this book. Did you think of an artist as someone with a special gift or skill or talent? Someone with their own personal muse on speed dial? Someone who makes good art?

In his book, *Orbiting the Giant Hairball*, Gordon McKenzie tells the story of teaching art to kids. In the first- and second-grade classes, when he would ask, "Who here is an artist?" every kid would eagerly raise and wave their hands. They could all point to the walls and show him paintings they had done and images they had created. By fifth grade, only a few students would cautiously raise their hands.

As we grow older, we begin to assume that only those people who can make art with exceptional skill, who bring a universal meaning to their work, or who have a strong natural talent in design or representational drawing deserve to be called artists. Yet the first graders get it intuitively: If they are doing the work of art, they are artists.

Our culture has gotten more and more specialized. Creative endeavors have become the domain of children and trained professionals. It used to be that anyone could sit around the campfire and sing. Sure, a few people were better at it, and maybe they led or did solos, but everyone else still got to pitch in on the chorus or take a turn leading a raucous drinking song. Now we're all like a bunch of fifth graders, afraid to raise our hands and sing out in case someone sneers and says, "You're no Frank Sinatra!"

The word *amateur* originally meant "one who loves something." Strangely, a lot of people think they shouldn't paint, sing, or write poems, especially if they've been told somewhere along the line that they're not particularly talented. I believe just the opposite. If you love it, do it. By doing it, you'll find your skill increasing. I deeply

> *Art is not a thing; it is a way.*
> –*Elbert Hubbard*

> *He who works with his hands is a laborer. He who works with his hands and his head is a craftsman. He who works with his hands and his head and his heart is an artist.*
> –*St. Francis of Assisi*

Definition

Artist *Noun:* Someone who, with their own level of skill and passion, intentionally makes things in a meaningful and mindful way; a person whose primary work is to find meaning and express it in concrete or tangible ways; an identity available to all of us as our birthright.

believe that we are all artists, each with our own level of skill and talent, each with our own truths to explore and express, our own conversations to engage in, and our own gifts to channel. Accessing that ability, whether in the context of our daily lives or a particular creative medium, is part of why we're here.

And it may still be true that artmaking may never be your primary or paid work. Not everyone who makes meaningful or even meaningful and beautiful art is going to be a professional artist. I am not a professional athlete. I don't have the natural physical talent (nor have I spent the time developing the skills) to be a professional athlete. However, I don't let that stop me from hiking, dancing, or doing yoga. It doesn't stop me from using and enjoying my body, and it doesn't stop me from getting stronger the more I practice.

Would you let the fact that you're not Lance Armstrong keep you from riding a bike in France? Would you let the fact that you're not Frank Sinatra keep you from raising your voice and doing it your way? Would you let the fact that you're not a priest keep you from praying?

Don't be afraid to be an artist—even part-time. If you love artmaking, be an amateur. To paraphrase Robert Shaw, art is too important to be left to professionals.

What Is Spirituality?

A great deal of time can be spent debating the nature of spirituality. In my experience, most people can agree that spirituality is not dependent on organized religion, though it certainly can be a part of religious life. Would you agree or disagree? What role has religion played in your life? What about spirituality? How would you define spirituality, if you consider it as separate from organized religion?

The way I frame spirituality has its roots in my experiences with 12-Step programs like Alcoholics Anonymous. Such programs ask you to acknowledge a Higher Power, to admit that there is something out there greater than you are. For some people, that "something greater" starts with the family unit, then extends out to a greater concept of humanity. For other people, it is best described in the natural world. Others find a deep, resonating truth in Judaism or Christianity that allows them to think beyond themselves, while others may find that in the traditions of Buddhism, Wicca, or Islam.

For me, that something greater is best described as a Divine energy or force that flows through all of us, connecting us in such a way that the Whole is greater than the sum of its parts. I tend to refer to this as Spirit or the Divine. For me, spirituality is both the acknowledgement of Spirit, and the actions that stem from that acknowledgement.

For the purposes of this book, it's not important how you describe that "something greater." What matters is that you are willing to consider the idea and explore it.

What Is Prayer?

When I was a child, I used to think of prayer as bowing my head in church while the preacher spoke, holding hands before a meal, or quickly chanting a plea for forgive-

---

Every artist was first an amateur.

–Ralph Waldo Emerson

The artist is not a special kind of person, but every person is a special kind of artist.

– A. K. Coomaraswamy

Music and sex are too important to leave to the professionals.

–Conductor Robert Shaw, as quoted in The Art of Possibility by R. S. and B. Zander

Definition

Spirituality *Noun:* The internal acknowledgement that there is something greater than our self, also called God, the Source, Spirit, Nature, the Divine, Higher Power, Love, Higher Self, Universal Oneness, Allah, Great Mother, and many other names; actions stemming from this internal acknowledgement.

ness and good grades before bed. What about you? What was prayer when you were younger? What about now?

Communication is the foundation for any good relationship, and communication is a two-way street. Traditionally, we tend to think of prayer as talking to God, and we think of meditation as clearing the mind (or quieting the ego) to accept or receive what comes. Praying is talking and meditating is listening.

My theory is that if you want to have a relationship with Spirit, you've got to be willing to communicate. Both ways. So when I use the word *prayer* in this book to describe communicating with Spirit, I mean both speaking and listening.

This may bring up questions about the nature of the Divine. If you think of Spirit in terms of a personal God, it seems logical to pursue a relationship. So what happens if you think of Spirit as an intangible energy, unknowable force, or abstract concept? How do you communicate with a concept?

In that instance, it's not so much communicating as it is connecting. Acknowledging that there is something greater than yourself, and that you are a part of it, and that it is a part of you. What happens if you cultivate an awareness of that connection? If you engage in activities that help you to feel—and honor—that oneness more deeply? In my experience, what happens is prayer. And artmaking is one way of engaging in the act of prayer.

Spiritual work is often described as a dynamic dance of will and surrender. We must take action or exert our free will and make choices in order for things to happen in the world, and, at the same time, we must surrender our illusion that we are in control of what happens in the world. The conversation that is prayer, and the conversation that is artmaking, are both exquisite exercises in this dance.

Why Playful?

At first, *playful* may seem like a strange word to use with prayer. Perhaps it's because the word has taken on a bad reputation. If something is playful, it's not serious enough, it's too flighty for something as weighty as communing with Spirit. Or is it?

Playing is a way of learning. It's an important part of how children learn, and it's a way of learning that we do naturally and that we enjoy. What if prayer—and art—were simply natural and enjoyable ways of learning about ourselves and the Divine?

Staying playful keeps us in the right frame of mind: authentic, spontaneous, and intuitive. Staying playful also reminds us that the dance of will and surrender is a dance, not drudgery.

Artmaking as playful prayer is making art as a spiritual practice.

Creative work is play. It is free speculation using materials of one's chosen form.

–Stephen Nachmanovitch

A Note to Those Who Say They Can't Draw

Yes, hello—you over there in the corner waving your hand and looking stressed out. "But I can't draw!" you're telling me.

"Really? You can't draw?

"I can't even draw a straight line!"

Well, I'm not going to ask you to draw any perfectly straight lines, and if you get a line as straight as it is in, oh, say the cross-bar of a cursive letter "T" then you'll be fine. If you can write your name, you've probably got all of the manual dexterity you need. And if you feel the strong need to make a straight line, we can find a ruler.

"But we're supposed to be making art, and all I can do is draw stick figures!"

Hey, if you can make stick figures, you're ahead of the game! Stick figures can actually be pretty expressive. I bet you could even draw a tree so that I would recognize it. It might not look like a photograph of a tree, but I bet you could draw a tree so that "tree" would be one of my first three guesses. Especially if I gave you a lot of time to do it and a tree to look at and a few different colors to draw it with. If you took some time and patience and care, I bet you could draw it well enough so that "tree" would be my first guess.

"Well, yeah, but . . ."

It might not look quite as good as the picture in your head, but I would know it was a tree. Most importantly, you would know it was a tree, right?

"I guess, but . . ."

And even if I didn't know or you were afraid someone might be confused, you could write "this is a tree" underneath it in large, clear letters.

"Well, that's a little silly . . ."

Or you could find a picture of a tree and trace it, or you could just cut out a picture of a tree and put it in the middle of the piece of paper and then, clearly, it would be a tree.

"Yes."

So, you would be able, one way or another, to communicate the idea of "tree" to me effectively.

"Yes."

Then you'd be able to get the meaning across, right?

"Yes."

Ok, that's what I thought. So, now you know, that in a pinch, you can get your ideas across visually even if you think you can't draw. And you know that you always have the option of using any of those techniques—really simple drawing with stick figures, tracing, writing, drawing from life, or collaging—in any of your artwork if you feel stuck.

Now, let's back up a bit, because the bottom line is that it doesn't matter if you communicate the idea of a tree. It doesn't matter if I know what it is. It really doesn't even matter if you know what it is. Even if you think you know what you've just drawn, your inner self will always know a lot more about what's going on. Because the point is the process and the process is prayer. You're here to discover, to follow the impulses, and to listen.

And if your impulse is to draw a tree, then do it! Don't question it or analyze it—and don't judge the result. Just follow the impulse. Too often when

THE CREATIVE CONVERSATION: ARTMAKING AS PLAYFUL PRAYER

we say "I can't draw" what we're really saying is "I don't trust myself to make it look the way it's supposed to look."

The truth is that there may be something beyond "tree" in what you have to draw. Maybe you're really loving the look of the green crayon, and maybe you start to draw a tree. Maybe the green squiggles or lines or leaf shapes feel really good to draw. Maybe the dark line of the trunk wants to go on forever and the roots want to reach back up into the sky...let go of the nagging little voice that might be saying "But that isn't how a tree is supposed to look." Draw the tree that's unique to you.

You may discover that you are drawing "the way the light fell through the branches of the willow in my backyard on late summer afternoons those years ago when I was growing up" or simply "I really like this shade of green and making squiggles feels really good." And it may change every few minutes. If you can let go of making a tree look like you think it's supposed to, you are free to follow those impulses wherever they may go.

You don't have to be able to draw recognizable things. You just need to be willing to show up and make the marks.

The creation of something new is not accomplished by the intellect but by the play instinct acting from inner necessity. The creative mind plays with the object it loves.

–Carl Jung

Thank goodness I was never sent to art school; it would have rubbed off some of the originality.

–Beatrix Potter

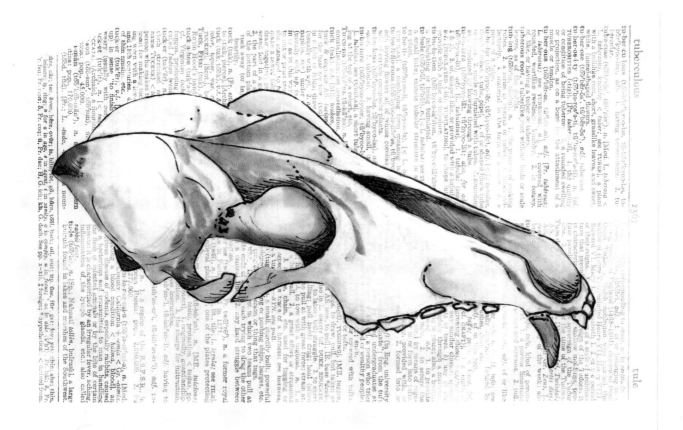

A Note to the Trained Artist

If you've had art training of any kind, you may feel challenged by the idea of letting go of the rules. You may hear your teacher whispering in your ear, telling you the right way to do it. If you make art for a living, you may find it extremely difficult to let go of creating for product. You may worry about putting so much time into pieces that aren't saleable. Or you may find that giving yourself over completely to process feels like a huge relief, especially after working for hours or days on commission work.

What's important to remember is that while your artmaking as playful prayer and your other artwork will inform and influence each other, they are not the same thing. Artwork made to submit to galleries or to perfect your technique are by their very nature product-focused rather than process-focused. Your intentions when you start working on them will be different than when you settle in to a session of artmaking as playful prayer.

As a professional artist, I spend a large part of my time working in a very product-oriented way. Yet even if I have a very product-oriented task such as "I will work on 15 pieces for this gallery show coming up" or "I will work from this sketch in my notebook" or even "I will make a birthday card for my boyfriend," I'll add a caveat. Including something like "and I'll have fun" or "I'm allowed to make mistakes" or "not every piece has to be perfect, it's a learning process" keeps me loose and integrates what I've learned in my spiritual practice more fully into my life.

When working on product-oriented pieces, I will frequently have several canvases going at once, so that I can hop from one to the other and not over-think, over-analyze, or attempt to over-perfect the piece that is the current focus of my attention. If I find myself getting stuck, I'll move to another piece, maybe one that doesn't matter as much or is more process-oriented and do some work on that one to re-energize.

Sometimes, too, I'll find myself bouncing back and forth between product and process in a single piece. Stepping into an artmaking-as-playful-prayer mindset can absolutely energize a product-oriented piece, much as getting too focused on product can stifle the energy in a process-oriented piece. Some artists fully trust every impulse and will show and sell pure process work. I believe much of what we call visionary art or even outsider art falls into this category, and this is part of why I find this work so compelling. Ultimately, only you will know what balance is right for you and what role artmaking as playful prayer will take in the work you show and sell.

Either way, I encourage you to devote at least some of your studio time to making art that is pure process, pure dialog between you and Spirit.

A Note to Everyone on Process vs. Product

Whether you're new to artmaking or an old pro, the pressure is always there to make something good. We want to produce something that we can show our friends rather than simply exploring, playing, or listening. In our culture, we tend to either put artists up on pedestals by saying "I wish I could be that creative!" or minimize their work by saying, "A child could do that!" So when we start to explore artmaking, we take the risk of either not living up to the standards of real art or looking like a foolish child.

The truth is closer to Pablo Picasso's quip: "Every child is an artist. The problem is how to remain an artist once we grow up." I believe that we start out as youngsters with finger paint and crayons and an incredible curiosity. Curiosity is critical to creativity; it is exploration without judgment. If we maintain a curious perspective as we work, we allow ourselves to be in the moment and to wonder what will happen next.

When I talk about process-oriented artmaking, I am talking about making art with this attitude of mindful curiosity. I am asking you to let go of your concerns about what others will think and your notions of what art is supposed to look like. To approach your art as a child might.

Just start making.

I said to myself, I have things in my head that are not like what anyone has taught me—shapes and ideas so near to me—so natural to my way of being and thinking that it hasn't occurred to me to put them down. I decided to start anew, to strip away what I had been taught.

–Georgia O'Keefe

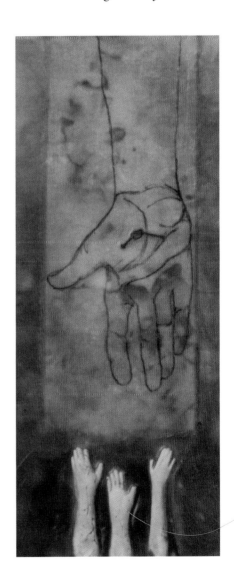

Blind Drawing

Materials

- Blank paper or sketchbook
- A simple, familiar object
- Pen or pencil

1. Find a simple, familiar object such as a mug, lamp or chair. Set yourself up where you can see the object and get your paper and pen ready. Position your pen on the paper and look at the object.

2. Now, without looking again at the paper, begin to draw what you see. Focus on what you see and recording those impulses through the movement of your hand and the pen. Don't look back at the paper, and don't lift the pen up off the paper. Just move your hand in response to your eyes as they follow the outline and curves and nooks of the object. Let your eyes caress and notice the object and let your hand express those visual caresses.

3. When you feel like you have visually examined every surface, stop moving the pen and look at the drawing. In some ways, it's a misnomer to call this a *blind drawing* because you are really deeply focused on seeing the subject of the drawing; you're simply not looking at the drawing itself until the very end. Now, consider the drawing not as a representation of the object, but simply as a record of your careful observation of the object.

Additional Materials

• Your favorite painting or coloring tools (colored pencils, crayons, chalk pastels, acrylics, tempera or watercolors)

While this exercise is complete in and of itself, you might consider adding color to the drawings after they're done. Now, instead of looking only at the object, put the object away and experiment with only looking at the image you've created.

Color is wonderful, and adding color to images can be a delightful process. And the color doesn't have to relate to reality. Try applying color without observing where it shows up in the object: Instead, let the color become a conversation with the lines that are there on the paper. A splash of orange might dance with that strong line, a swath of yellow make that interesting shape stand out, or use magenta just because it makes you happy.

Visual Definitions

Materials

- Blank paper or sketchbook
- Junk mail or old magazines
- Scissors or craft knife
- Glue stick
- Brayer or old gift card

1. Begin by considering the terms I defined in this chapter: *art, artist, spirituality, prayer* and *playful*. Was there one you were particularly drawn to or struggled with? Take a moment to sit quietly with the word that holds the most energy for you. Take a few moments to write out your own definition of the word or your thoughts on what that word means to you.

2. Now, let go of the word and turn to your stack of junk mail, old magazines, or other collage materials. Take 15 minutes and pull out images, words, colors, and textures that you are attracted to, that grab your attention or that hold a lot of energy for you. Don't analyze your choices or self-edit.

3. At the end of 15 minutes, create a collage using only the images you selected. COLLAGE TIP: If you want your collage elements to lie smoothly on the paper, try using the edge of an old gift card to smooth and flatten them. This works best when you are using a glue stick or there's no glue on the surface of the collage.

4. Remember that by letting go of the word before you start working on the collage, you're freeing up your intuition to help you choose the images. You're not trying to make a collage about art: You're just involved in the process of making a collage after you've been thinking about art. This (phew!) releases you from any particular product, while still giving you a chance to see if anything new or interesting comes out of the process.

Additional Materials
- Pen or pencil
- Journal or notepad

A. When you feel done with the collage, ask yourself, "What does this collage have to tell me about the word I meditated on? How are the images I selected related to my own attitudes and baggage around that word?" Spend some time journaling on the questions.

B. Consider doing this collage process for each of the words defined in this chapter.

Chapter 3
Studio: Making Sacred Space for ArtMaking

Making Room for Art at Home

It is one thing to go off to an art class once a week and another to work alone at home. In the class, there are other people taking the same risks you are. There are supplies to choose from and a space to work in and permission to make a mess. You know that when you come back the next week, the supplies and the space will be there. There is a teacher or facilitator who is cheering you on, giving you ideas and information about materials, and, I hope, setting guidelines that make the space a safe and fun place for everyone to explore. Yet even if you're blessed with having a great workshop environment, you'll end up wanting to do some work at home or in your own studio space.

Over the years, I've gone from having a corner workspace in my bedroom, to the use of larger spaces in a variety of mildew-prone basements, to the glorious converted two-car garage I now call my studio home. Some full-time and part-time artists rent studio space outside of their home, and some continue to work for years from that corner in the bedroom. Whether the space is in your house or not, you want to have at least some space that is yours alone and not used for any other purpose.

Ideally, you want to have a space where you can leave your supplies set up and works in progress out and visible. This way, you can sit down and work for a few minutes here and there, and you are always walking by your project—catching it out of the corner of your eye and letting your subconscious work on it too. It keeps your artist self out and visible and taking up space; it identifies artmaking as as much of a priority as sleeping, cooking, or bathing. It becomes as easy to add a bit of color to a piece as it does to heat up leftovers in the microwave, check email, or flip on the TV.

The reality is that in the beginning, your workspace will probably be in your house, and you will probably share your house with other people who may or may not understand what you're doing. Your home may be small and you might not feel like you have any space to claim for art, or that the spaces in your home are too "public" for the purpose. You may have children or housemates who would take great delight in using your art supplies, and you may find that they do not have the same notions of privacy or respect for materials and works-in-progress that you might need. You might be working on things that you simply don't want other people to see.

For a bare-bones home studio, all you need is something to make marks with, something to make marks on, and a place to be while you make those marks. Here are some ideas for setting up a studio in a small or shared space:

THE ONE-WALL STUDIO

I once met a woman who had simply dedicated one wall of her kitchen to painting. It wasn't a large space and yet she had made room for herself. She had tacked cardboard to the wall and floor to protect it, hung heavy paper on the wall to paint on, and then had a tray with her paints on it that could be easily repositioned. It was always there, and it was easy for her to step in and paint without the production of setting up her space each time she wanted to work.

THE STUDIO BEHIND THE COUCH

A friend once described seeing the studio of a professional printmaker she knew and being shocked by its simplicity. The artist had moved the couch in his tiny living room away from the big front window, and placed a table and a few shelves behind it. There

was room to walk between the table and the window, and everything he needed to do his work was within easy reach and always ready to go. This setup had made his living room smaller, but it also made his priorities very clear!

Is there a space, like your living room or bedroom, that you could shrink slightly in order to make room for a small studio space? How could you rearrange an existing room so that a little space for art is carved out? Don't forget that basements and garages are frequently overlooked and underused spaces that can be made much more pleasant with the addition of a little paint and some well-placed lights. Fans, heaters, and houseplants can also go a long way towards making a space more welcoming.

THE FOLD-OUT STUDIO IN A CLOSET

Claim a guest room closet, hall closet, coat closet, or linen closet for your studio. You probably need to get rid of a few things anyway, and a little re-arranging can find a new home for the items that are still left. If the closet doesn't have a light, a clip lamp and an extension cord can solve that problem. Use the closet to hold your art supplies and a bulletin board or other "display" area for inspirational images and quotes, works in process, and even completed projects.

If you paint, try hanging the piece you're working on the back of the door and keep a folding chair in the closet. Open the door, secure it with a couple of rubber wedges to keep it from moving, and voilà!—you have an easel. Or if you work on a horizontal surface and stand while you work, try getting a fold-down ironing board for the back of the door. This can fold down and become an instant work surface! If your door is solid wood rather than hollow-core, you might try one of the wall-mount fold-down tables available at stores like IKEA. If you sit while you work on a horizontal surface, you can try using one of the shelves in the closet as a work surface, or find a small table that fits the space. Or you can keep a folding table in the closet, and display works in progress and inspiring quotes on the door.

The idea is to create a space that you can close the door on, and that is ready to go with supplies on hand and works in process that are visible as soon as you open the door to set up the work surface. You can also leave the door open and your projects in process visible for those times when you want to keep your subconscious at work.

STUDIO IN A TUB

Keep all of your art supplies and projects in plastic bins, totes, or tubs that can be easily carried and stored. This is especially handy if your primary workspace is the dining

THE CREATIVE CONVERSATION: ARTMAKING AS PLAYFUL PRAYER

room table or a card table set up in the living room. This makes it easy to clear the room and relocate the project somewhere else or just put it away until dinner is over. Tubs can be organized by media or by project.

STUDIO ON A CART

A similar idea is to keep your art supplies on a rolling cart, like a kitchen utility cart or catering cart. Some are designed as rolling kitchen islands, others to hold microwaves or TVs. These carts frequently have a drawer and usually have at least one shelf. I've seen very sturdy rolling tool carts at hardware stores that have multiple shallow drawers, ideal for paints, pastels, paper, and brushes. Sometimes the cabinets underneath can be easily covered with fabric, or have doors—great for privacy! The top surface can be used to store works in process and can even be used as a work surface.

I keep all of my painting supplies on a cart like this. Roll it up to the kitchen table, or to an easel, or even out onto the back porch, and you're ready to go. If the dining table is your main work surface, it's easy to turn the dining nook into a sometime studio. You can keep a bulletin board on a wall nearby full of inspiring pictures and quotes, or have a magnet board to easily display finished projects. Keep your rolling cart full of supplies in the dining room and stock it with a vinyl tablecloth or piece of oilcloth that you can throw down on the dining room table to protect the surface. Then roll your cart over, sit down, and dive in! Your supplies are near at hand, and cleaning up your work surface in time for dinner is as simple as folding up the vinyl cloth and putting your project on top of the cart—where your subconscious can again work on it over coffee and pie.

THE JOURNAL

In many ways, the first stages of artmaking as playful prayer, which involve finding internal clarity, exploring, and playing, are the stuff of journals. We are journaling in paint, in found images, in scribbles and doodles of pen and pencil, recording a visual stream of consciousness. Since artmaking as playful prayer is about engagement in process, not product, a private diary is a great place to keep your projects.

A sketchpad with heavy weight sketch paper is ideal (one that you can use for watercolor and markers as well as pencil, at least 60# paper), and they come in a lot of different sizes. Get one that will be large enough for you to really feel free in—I have one that's 9" × 9" for doing mandalas, and another one that's 9" × 12" for everyday stuff. Both these sizes are easy to slip in a drawer, toss in the car, or tuck in a backpack. Next, pack a pencil bag with some markers, colored pencils, a travel water color set, small scissors, and glue stick, or whatever tools you regularly use. Keep it with the sketchbook, and wherever you are becomes your studio.

Making It Sacred Space

Because we are looking at artmaking as a spiritual practice as well as a fun, playful, and potentially messy activity, you will want to make sure that your art space also supports a spiritual connection. Because each person's connection to Spirit is unique, so too will be the things that make your artmaking space feel like sacred space to you. Here are some things you can try.

> **Definition**
>
> **Sacred** *Adj:* Dedicated to or set apart for connection with the Divine; dedicated or devoted exclusively to a single use, purpose, or person; worthy of reverence or respect; not secular or profane; something that, because of its unique qualities or symbolic value, allows us to more easily or directly make a spiritual connection.

BRINGING THE ELEMENTS IN

Altars from many spiritual traditions include a token representing each of the elements: earth, air, fire, and water. I generally find that an altar or focusing point will feel more complete if I have a stone, feather, candle, and sea shell or other natural symbols of the elements included in it. The same may be true for your artmaking space. Try bringing in rocks, moss, pine cones, flowers, shells, feathers, roots, leaves, or other interesting bits of nature that you find on walks.

Working in a space that has windows, a collection of natural objects, or a calendar full of outdoor scenes may put you back in touch with the natural rhythms that we all dance to. A plant, a bowl of fruit, a birdfeeder outside the window, or even the presence of a studio cat may be enough to remind you of your connection with the natural world.

WELCOME THE GUIDES

I have a friend whose studio is full of images of the Virgin Mary. These images of the compassionate mother are both soothing and supportive to her in her work. I have images of the Hindu goddesses Sarisvati and Kali in my studio. The gentle wise goddess of knowledge, art, poetry, and teaching and the fiercely protective demon-destroying mother goddess watch over me as I work, and they remind me of my mission to serve as a creative spark and to harness my fiery passion for good works. Your guides may be Divine figures or they may be admired artists, writers, spiritual leaders, thinkers, or loved ones. I encourage you to include images of those who inspire you to embody your best self in your work space. Note: If your faith tradition would interpret these as graven images, consider using an inspiring quote instead.

SETTING THE TONE

Some people are very sensitive to sound. It can create mood and set a tone. Simply turning on a favorite CD of chants, flute music, or nature sounds can subtly shift your frame of mind. You might choose to incorporate drumming, chanting, singing, or other music-making into your artmaking routine, or you may find that silence is the most powerful sound of all. Keeping a bell or chime near your artmaking space and ringing it before you start in to work can also literally set the tone.

ACTIVATE THE SENSES

Smell is one of our most primal senses, and it connects us strongly with emotion and memory. Choose a scent that reminds you of a particularly powerful spiritual connection: fresh pine needles, warm cinnamon, tangy citrus, sweet jasmine, or comforting vanilla. Find a candle or incense that embodies that scent, and light it when you get ready to start work. There may be an incense blend like Nag Champa or Patchouli that sets the mood for you; or you may find a room spray made with essential oils that does the trick. Smudging with sage can also leave a room feeling cleansed.

WORDS OF WISDOM

Print out a few favorite inspirational quotes, Bible verses, or poems and hang them in your space. You may also choose to write out your intention or affirmation and hang it where it can serve as a constant visual reminder.

Of course, you can fill a space with objects and images and words and scents and sounds, and still find that it lacks any spiritual connection for you. While all of these things can help set a space apart, make it special and signify that important work is being done, a quote or a special candle are little more than reminders of why you're there. They alone do not create the space; they simply provide what Buddhists call "mind support." The most important components of making a space that will support artmaking as a spiritual practice have to do with your attitudes and intentions.

Two Key Attitudes That Help Make Sacred Space

A WILLINGNESS TO BE A NOVICE

The first time I walked into St. Peter's Basilica in Vatican City, I was overwhelmed by the time, energy, faith, and absolute devotion that had gone into creating the building. As I listened to the gentle sounds of the choir and gazed at the paintings and the stained glass, I was humbled. I finally realized how little I knew about Christianity in general and Catholicism in particular, and I realized that everything I thought I knew had almost nothing to do with the actual experience of a true believer. In that moment, I was a novice. Simply being there was enough to remind me that what I thought I knew was useless. In that moment, I was teachable.

Everyone starts somewhere. Whether you have been engaged in visual artmaking for years or have never picked up a brush before, you are now starting something new. You will now be making art for the process of making art, for the experience of making art, for the sheer joy of color and shape. You are not making art to make something good or even something beautiful. This is not about listening to your ego and this is not about speaking from your ego; this is about listening for the voice of Spirit and answering.

It is so easy to get caught up in whether we're doing something right, or whether our project looks like the one in the book, or whether the teacher likes us. If we bring the humble attitude that being in the process of artmaking is enough, that being

> **Definition**
>
> **Novice** *Noun:* A beginner, a student; a person new to a given field; a member of a religious order who has not yet taken final vows; one dedicated to a process of learning.

> *Courage is what it takes to stand up and speak; courage is also what it takes to sit down and listen.*
>
> *–Winston Churchill*

where we are is enough, then we are moving towards being in sacred space. And what a relief it is! We don't have to be perfect. We don't have to be doing it well. We simply have to show up and play. And, with any luck, we've got a quote or an image or some soothing music nearby to remind us to do just that.

A WILLINGNESS TO DEFER JUDGMENT

Stewart Cubley, co-author of *Life, Paint, and Passion*, uses the no-comment rule in his Painting Experience workshops. Participants are not allowed to comment on each other's work; they are only allowed to look. Pat B. Allen uses a similar guideline in her workshops. I generally use it too when I'm running a process-oriented class, or I give students the option of instituting the no-comment rule when discussing or sharing their work. It can be such a relief knowing that we can make things, and while someone may ask us a question about our process like "How's it going today?" or "How did you get that effect?" no one will say "I like that" or "I wish mine looked like that" or "What's that supposed to be?" In a group setting, the idea is that we are there to learn from ourselves and to learn from each other. We are not there to judge each other. Nor are we there to judge ourselves.

In creating a sacred artmaking space, we need to defer our judgment. There will be times to be engaged and to be discerning. This is not, however, the time for judgment. Save judgment for later. Again, we must be like the novice. We must have absolute faith in our lack of knowledge, and remember that our opinions do not serve us in this situation.

In order to keep your home workspace judgment-free, try instituting a no-comment rule in your house. Keep a tip jar by your art space, with a sign on it that says, "No comments—$1 fine" or "Each comment costs $1" as a way to enforce or encourage compliance— and raise funds for more art supplies! Another way to approach this is to simply request that instead of positive comments or constructive feedback, well-wishers can support you by contributing to an art supply fund or taking over a chore to give you more time to work!

Of course, keeping the external environment free of judgment is much easier than keeping the internal environment clear. The real trick is keeping your inner judge in check. If I had a tip jar for my internal critic, we could each afford to buy our own tropical island and never bother each other again! To date, however, my inner critic has not agreed to drop a single dime in the tip jar. No, we've had to learn how to get along. Later in the book, I'll offer more specific advice on communicating with these uncooperative inner voices.

Definition

Judgment *Noun:* The act of making a decision based on firm knowledge and evidence; the product of such a decision; that which happens when we behave as if we are in possession of greater knowledge or deeper truth than those around us; the result of behaving as if our opinion matters.

Take the attitude of a student, never be too big to ask questions, never know too much to learn something new.

– Og Mandino

Artful Explorations: Defer Judgment

Both of these Explorations are time-intensive. They can be done in small increments over the course of several days or weeks if you want.

Glue Doodle

Materials

- Patience and time
- Blank paper or sketchbook pages (larger and heavier is better, watercolor paper or bristol board is ideal)
- Elmer's glue (the non-washable kind is best for this)
- Watercolors
- Brushes and container of water
- Rag or paper towel
- Crayons or colored pencils

OPTIONAL
- Blue painter's tape
- Sanding block or sandpaper

1. To begin, open up the Elmer's glue (or some other white, fluid glue in a squeeze bottle) and start drawing with it. Just tip it over, squeeze, and doodle. Let go of how it looks. Fill up one page, then set it aside to dry and start working on another one. Go for quantity over quality. Try moving your arm from the shoulder, then the elbow, then the wrist, and see how the glue lines on the page change. Hold the glue bottle far away from the page to draw, then try moving it closer. Next, try drawing with the tip touching the paper. Make loops and doodles and swoops. Make lines, drops, drips. Draw squares on top of circles on top of triangles on top of stars or fill a page with a single pattern.

2. Now, let all the glue dry. This is the tough part. Set them aside overnight and let them dry completely before you do anything else. Patience, and letting things be ready for the next step, is a part of any artistic process. Push things too fast, and you get a sticky mess.

3. Once the pieces are dry, choose two or three of the glue drawings that are most appealing and lay them out on a table in front of you. To keep the paper from curling too much when you start adding the watercolor in the next step, you can tape it down to your work surface using the painter's tape. Unless you're using watercolor board, be careful not to get the paper too wet: Many papers will start disintegrating if attacked too ferociously with water and brush.

4. Take out your watercolors and wet your brush. Pick a color intuitively from the watercolor pan, dip the brush in, and brush some color on the paper. If the glue is completely dry, it will act as a resist to the watercolor. Some watercolor will adhere to the glue, but it will be a bit lighter. You'll also find that color will pool near the glue lines, emphasizing them. If you have too much water on the paper, blot with a rag or paper towel. Keep selecting and applying colors until you've filled all of the pages. Let go of making it look good. Let go of your opinions of the piece. Simply move from page to page as the impulse strikes.

5. Now, let the watercolor dry. Yup. More patience.

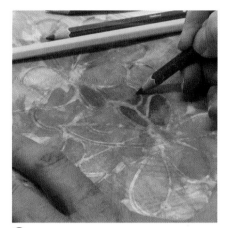  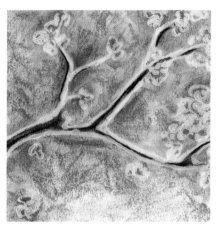

6. When the watercolor is dry, choose one of the pieces you painted. Gather up your crayons or colored pencils (or both!) and begin adding more intense, defined colors to some of the shapes. If you're using both colored pencils and crayons, keep in mind that crayon may go on over colored pencil, but colored pencil won't really make a mark on the waxy surface of the crayon. You may want to add patterns or doodles in the shapes or outline the lines made with the glue. Use the watercolor-painted glue doodle like a giant, abstract, intuitive coloring book. Enjoy intuitively deciding what color goes where and how dark or light, patterned or smooth, defined or vague each area needs to be.

7. When the piece is dry, you can also go over it lightly with some sandpaper. This will sand some of the color from the glue, highlighting those areas. Keep working until you feel done, going back into the piece with different media, then do the same for a few more of the pieces.

The challenge with this project is to keep working without worrying about whether it looks good or bad, to keep working without letting your opinion get in the way. See if you can enjoy the color and the line without judging or labeling the outcome. After all, it's a big glue doodle! Who knows what it is! Deferring judgment makes staying in the process that much easier.

Additional Materials
- Chalk pastels

OPTIONAL
- Workable fixative or hairspray
- Makeup sponges or applicators (fingers will work just fine)

It's possible to get some really interesting effects using chalk pastels over a dry glue doodle. The chalk hardly clings to the glue at all, making the white lines of the pattern stand out very strongly. Try drawing into the patterns with chalk pastels, using your fingers or a makeup sponge to blend colors. When you feel complete, spray the piece lightly with a workable fixative or hairspray to keep the pastel from smearing.

Layer It Up

This is one of the few projects designed specifically for use with acrylic paints and collage materials, because of the unique way that those materials interact with one another and can be layered. If you do not have acrylic paints, you may want to wait until you do before trying this one.

Materials

- Patience and time
- Junk mail or old magazines
- Blank paper or sketchbook (larger and heavier is better, watercolor board or bristol board is ideal)
- Gesso
- Gel medium or Mod Podge (matte medium or soft gel gloss medium is recommended though Mod Podge can be used)
- Acrylic paints
- Small and large brushes
- Container of water
- Rag or paper towels
- Permanent markers or ballpoint pens
- Scissors or craft knife

OPTIONAL
- Sanding block or sandpaper
- Blue painter's tape
- Rubbing alcohol in a spray bottle
- Blow dryer (to speed drying)
- Wax paper or palette
- Gift card or credit card

One of the great things about deferring judgment and focusing on process is that unexpected things happen. Combining and layering media is one way to jumpstart the unexpected and break up your own expectations. This layering work can serve as a background for journaling or other drawings or paintings, can be cut up and used in collage, or can be an end in itself.

1. Start with several pieces of heavy blank paper. It can be a good idea to work simultaneously on several pieces. This allows you to work on one piece while another is drying, meaning you don't have to completely stop working when a piece is wet! To keep the paper from curling up, you can tape it down to your work surface with the painter's tape.

2. LAYER ONE: Start by layering some collage materials. Try mixing more abstract and patterned papers like old dress patterns, sheets of music, and credit card bills in with more representational images like pictures from magazines. For this project, use gel medium as an adhesive. Lay down a thin layer of gel medium with a brush, then lay down your collage materials on top of the glue. Finally, coat all the collage pieces with another layer of gel medium. Let it dry.

COLLAGE TIP: Using gel medium or Mod Podge to adhere and seal your collage means that you can apply acrylic paints right on top of it and still get smooth paint application and even color despite the variety of papers you've used in your collage. However, the paper tends to get more wrinkled using this process.

Before you apply your topcoat, you can use a brayer or old credit card or gift card to smooth out the wrinkles in the paper. Start at the center of the image or collage piece and work outward. This also squeezes excess glue out from under the image, so use a tool that can get covered in glue.

Laying a piece of wax paper over the image first will help with the glue mess, but the wax paper will occasionally stick to a gluey bit and pull up part of the image. If you can stand the mess, you can do what I do: After I've put on the top coat, I use my fingers to smooth out wrinkles. Fingers slide well in the gluey mess, and I just clean up afterwards with a damp rag. I still end up with a lot of wrinkles, but I really love the texture!

 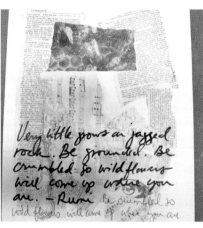 

LAYER TWO: Mix a little gesso with water—about half and half—or dip the tip of a very wet brush into your gesso. Now, brush it over the whole surface of your collage. Using a rag or paper towel, wipe some of it off, revealing the collage underneath. Let it dry.

LAYER THREE: Using a permanent marker like a Sharpie or even a ballpoint pen, write on the surface. You can write a poem, do some free-association journaling, write a grocery list, or write one word over and over. Just get some text in there. Let it dry.

LAYER FOUR: Now add some color. You can thin your acrylic paint with some gel medium, and brush it over the collage or use it more opaquely in select areas. Use several colors if you like. Before it dries, you can also try spritzing it with rubbing alcohol. This can cause the acrylic to separate in interesting ways. If you don't like it, blot it with a paper towel. Let it dry.

LAYER FIVE: Collage more materials onto the surface using gel medium as your adhesive. Let it dry.

LAYER SIX: Brush diluted gesso over the surface again, wiping some back. You can also paint the gesso on full strength or more precisely in some areas. Let it dry.

LAYER SEVEN: Wad up the paper, crumpling it. Unfold it, smooth it, and run over the surface lightly with sandpaper or sanding block.

LAYER EIGHT: Add a wash or two of color. The color will highlight the sanded areas. Use a rag to wipe off what you don't want.

LAYER NINE: Highlight or define certain areas. Use color and line to unify the piece. Try writing to add a little more text, drawing patterns, darkening the color in certain areas, or adding lines or dots. Use a permanent marker or acrylic paints.

3. Consider these questions: What kinds of effects did you get? What surprised you? What areas are most visually interesting?

TAKING IT FURTHER

Want to take it further? Keep adding layers. Rip up the sheets you've been working on, glue them to yet another sheet, and then keep adding layers. Build a collage, drawing, or painting on top of what's already happened. Write a poem on the sheet. Cut out shapes (try using cookie cutters as guides) and use them in a different collage.

A Conversation with Judgment and Process

There's a difference between deferring judgment and not caring about what you're doing. Working with both of these Explorations, you had to be careful, you had to respect the materials and their limits, and you had to make decisions. You did it in spite of the fact that your brain was probably full of all kinds of crazy talk.

At various points in the book, you'll be asked to do some journaling, ask yourself some questions, talk to your painting, or otherwise engage in conversation designed to let your inner voice speak up. The idea is to acknowledge and then get past the crazy talk, judgments, and old habits so that we can tap into the voice of Spirit. The simplest way to start is by grabbing a journal or a notepad, writing out the questions, and then just recording whatever pops into your head in response. Keep going, and your inner voice will have a chance to speak up.

Let's start. Look at the two or three pieces you've done. You've probably come to a sense of completion with each of them. You may even be pretty excited by how they came out, even though they just started out as a mess of glue or collaged images. I'd like you to go back now and think about thoughts and feelings that came up during the process:

- Did you have any doubts, judgments, or criticisms of yourself or the piece while you were working on it? What were they?
- How did those thoughts make you feel?
- What did you do when those thoughts and feelings came up? How did you respond to those thoughts and feelings?
- Now, look at the finished pieces. Do you still hear any of those doubts, judgments, or criticisms? How much do they matter now that the piece is complete?

You may find that the glue drip you thought was a huge mistake has become your favorite part of the piece, or that the crumpling you were afraid to do actually made the piece more interesting. All artists go through moments of doubt and frustration. And they keep working, working through the doubt and frustration. Sometimes, a piece you struggled with the most will become your favorite, or a process that you fought the hardest will turn out to have had the greatest rewards. Be ready to acknowledge those feelings when they come up, and then be ready to keep working anyway.

Seduced by Materials

One of the most delightful and intimidating things about making art is the materials. Oh, the brilliant colors of the pastels and the paints, the thousands of different types of papers, the soft sable brushes, the markers arranged like rainbows. It feels like a whole world of possibility and beauty is spread out before you … if only you can understand it and then afford to pay for it.

Our cave-dwelling ancestors started out with a rock wall, burnt sticks, and chalky stones. And the modern equivalent—taking a permanent marker and starting in on the living room wall—is just as simple and just as fun! However, if you have a picky landlord or are interested in maintaining the resale value of your home, you may want to explore some of the other equally simple and equally fun options coming up.

What You Need

All of the Artful Explorations start with really simple materials: paper and pen, scissors and glue, color and shape. Everything you need to get started is included in the list of Basic Materials below. You may be surprised by how much of it you already have. I've also made a list of suggested Intermediate Materials that will give you everything you need to complete the Artful Explorations, as well as many of the Taking It Further sections. A few of the Explorations include additional common household materials that you can easily find at a grocery store or tucked away in your cupboards.

In some cases I've recommended sizes and even brands, things that my students and I have had good experiences with. However, that doesn't mean you can't substitute, and it certainly doesn't mean you need to go out and spend a lot of money on art supplies. In fact, I suggest that you don't spend money on materials from the Intermediate list until you've read through the projects that suggest those materials and made your own determination about whether you want or need them.

I also include a list of Extra Materials. These are things that I find myself using in my own mixed-media explorations, things that come in handy as the projects grow more involved. They will also allow you to explore ideas for taking the Artful Explorations further, and a few of these items made their way into samples in this book. There's no need to rush out and buy any of these things. However, if you already have some of them, you may enjoy using them to expand your own Explorations.

Daunted by Glue or Color?

If you are new to artmaking and the idea of working with color leaves you confused or if you have limited experience using paints, you may find the information about color on my website, www.eyesaflame.com, useful as it gives you a basic color wheel and information on mixing colors and using acrylic paints. I also include a brief overview of different water-based paints in the Intermediate Materials section.

In each of the sections, I suggest a variety of glues, adhesives, and fasteners. I also suggest using different types of glues in each of the Explorations. If you are intimidated by the huge variety of glues out there (and who hasn't been!), be sure to check out the information on adhesives on my website, www.eyesaflame.com under the resources section, which has lots of useful information on different adhesives and when to use them.

Basic Materials

This is all you need to get started on the Artful Explorations in each chapter. In fact, you may find that this kit and a little ingenuity is all you'll ever need. You probably already have several of these items, and if you don't, less than $25 at a discount store or craft store should get you everything on the list with change left over. Find a sturdy athletic shoe box, plastic bin, or bag to store your materials, and you're ready to go.

Of course, as you continue, you may find it worthwhile to invest in higher-quality paints, paper, or brushes.

- **A few cheap foam or bristle brushes**, ¼" to 2" wide
- **A few smaller bristle brushes**, in a variety of shapes, round and flat
- **A jar or old yogurt tub** to hold water for painting
- **Rags or paper towels**

- **A pair of sharp scissors**
- **A glue stick**
- **A bottle of Elmer's® Glue** or other fluid white glue
- **A pencil with eraser**
- **An old credit card or gift card** to use as a squeegee
- **A black Sharpie® pen** or other permanent marker
- **A ballpoint pen**

- **A journal or lined notepad**
- **Paper** Plain white typing or copier paper will work to start, as will newsprint or a cheap sketchbook. If you can invest the money, I recommend a 9" × 12" sketchpad with 60# paper.
- **A pad of colored construction paper** or origami papers without patterns

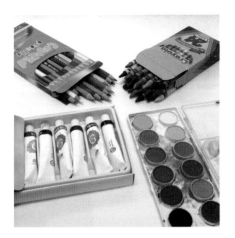

- **Something to make lines and shapes of color with** This might be markers, a box of crayons, or a selection of colored pencils—I'm especially fond of crayons and colored pencils! Crayola® makes a lot of inexpensive, good-quality art supplies.
- **A set of inexpensive pan watercolors**

- **Old magazines, books, greeting cards, catalogs, old telephone books, and junk mail for collage** A trip to a thrift store or a local yard sale can get you a stack of old magazines and picture books for a few dollars to get started, and then you can just start saving your old calendars, greeting cards, magazines and junk mail. You'll be amazed at how quickly you build up an impressive collage stash.
- **Old cereal boxes or scrap cardboard** These make great surfaces for collage or other projects. Cereal boxes work especially well—just flatten the boxes and trim them down so you can use the two largest panels. If you don't have heavy paper, sometimes a scrap of cardboard coated with gesso will do the trick.
- **An eye constantly peeled for other random household, thrift store, yard sale, and dollar store junk as needed** Old boxes, old books, toilet paper tubes, string, used twist ties, yarn, fabric scraps, glitter, sequins, pom-poms, plastic veggie tubs, snapshots, holiday cards, plastic bags, rubber bands, sponges, buttons, matchboxes…you get the idea. As you work through the book, be open to ways that your discards can turn into your art.

A Note about Copyrighted Materials

Many of the projects in this book encourage you to make photocopies of found images or use images ripped from magazines in your artmaking. Generally, if you are doing this at home for your own personal use or in an educational setting, there are no problems with using such found images in your artwork. It's considered fair use and you're not profiting from the original artist's work in any way.

However, it's only fair to warn you that using found images (i.e., someone else's copyrighted artwork) and then publicly displaying, reproducing, or selling that work has the potential to open up a big legal can of worms. I have been careful to use my own photographs, art in the public domain, and images for which I have permission in the examples in this book. If any copyrighted images made their way in, it was an unfortunate oversight on my part, and I apologize. Similarly, I would ask you to be respectful in your use of the images you find in this book.

If you have any concerns about using found images, limit your use to images that are in the public domain or that include permissions for use (this includes many clip art products from Dover Publications,). If you want to reproduce or sell work that includes copyrighted images like mine, check with a lawyer. I'm an artist, not an expert on copyright law, so please just consider this a friendly heads-up and not legal advice.

Intermediate Materials

Adding these items will round out your art supply selection and allow you to complete all of the more in-depth Artful Explorations in this book. I suggest that you do a little experimenting with the basic materials before you invest in these more expensive items. Also, don't feel like you have to get all of them at once—try materials one at a time, or in small groups, and see what you like best.

- **A large sketchpad or pad of paper**—at least 9" × 12"—with medium to heavy-weight sketch paper. You want to be able to use things like watercolors, markers, and paint on it as well as using pencil—look for paper that's labeled for these uses or that is at least 60#.
- **A pad of bristol board or 90# watercolor paper**—at least 8" × 10"

- **A set of acrylic paints** I go into great detail about acrylic paints in the resources section of my website, www.eyesaflame.com. Acrylics are wonderfully flexible paints, and there are many great manufacturers out there. I tend to use paints from Golden® because they are high quality, easy to find, and provide a great telephone help line if you have questions about using their products. Since I have them around, they are what I used in the Explorations and what appear in the accompanying photographs.

- **Acrylic matte medium and/or acrylic soft gel medium** This can be used as both a glue and a medium for your acrylic paints.
- **A jar of white acrylic gesso** Gesso is like a primer for any surface you're going to paint—it covers up what's underneath and gives you a smooth, slightly absorbent surface to work on. Painting on cardboard, like an old cereal box? A little gesso can make it feel like a much nicer painting surface!
- **A few good brushes, including a round brush, a flat brush, and a pointed or detail brush** These often come in inexpensive starter sets—those labeled for water-based media like acrylic or watercolor are your best bets. Generally, brushes for acrylic will be a bit stiffer than those for watercolor, and some artists find they offer more control.

- **Tubes of more richly pigmented watercolors, tubes of gouache, or jars of tempera paints (also called poster paints or kid's paints)** All of these are water-based paints, work well on paper, and are very easy to use. What makes them different is how opaque they are. Also, when it comes to paint, generally the more expensive the paint is, the more pigment it has. This means you'll be able to get bolder color with less product when you're using more expensive paints. After you've played with the $1.99 set of watercolors, you may want to upgrade your watercolors—or you may want to invest in some inexpensive gouache or temperas and see what that's like to play with more opaque colors. I like having these in addition to acrylics, though if you have to choose only one to invest money in, I'd pick the acrylics. You can use acrylics for an Exploration that calls for tempera or gouache, but the reverse is not necessarily true.

Watercolors are very transparent. When you're painting, you start off with the lightest colors, then build up to dark colors. It can be very tricky to get precise shapes and clear colors, though it is probably one of the least expensive mediums on this list.

Gouache can be both semi-transparent if it's watered down or quite opaque straight from the tube. A small tube will go a long way. It's very flexible, and it's my favorite type of paint to take with me when I travel.

Tempera or poster paint is very opaque and it dries quickly. It's generally non-toxic, so it's also great if you're painting with your hands. You can lay the color on fairly thick, though it will chip off if it's too thick. It also remains water-soluble, even when dry, so building up layers of paint can be a challenge. Using artist's grade temperas mitigates some of these problems, though they can be more expensive and more difficult to find. In spite of these minor limitations, jars of tempera remain my favorite for process painting and large, quick, expressive work.

- **Mod Podge®**
- **A hot glue gun and glue sticks**
- **Blue painter's tape** Masking tape will work, but blue painter's tape or low tack painter's tape has the best adhesion to and easy release from paper that I've found.
- **A thick, non-toxic craft glue** like Aleene's® Tacky Glue® or Crafter's Pick™ The Ultimate Glue
- **A heavy-duty adhesive** like E6000® or Amazing Goop®

- **A roll of wax paper or parchment paper** I've found that sheets of waxed deli paper also work really well. I use these sheets as paint palettes and as a way of protecting surfaces.
- **A craft knife, like an x-acto™ knife, and extra blades** I'd rather spend the money on new blades than carpel tunnel surgery.
- **A self-healing cutting mat** to use with your craft knife
- **A metal ruler with a cork pad backing** Most metal rulers come this way, and they make great straight edges that won't mar your paper or your art surface.
- **Fine or extra-fine sandpaper** or sanding block
- **String or yarn**

Extra Materials

As you move deeper into your artmaking, you may want to try some of the alternative techniques described for taking it further in the Artful Exploration projects. While these things can make your work go more easily and can allow you to do some more interesting experimentation, you don't need them to do any of the projects in this book. If you've already got some of these things on hand, marvelous!

- **A few rubber stamps with images that are symbolic or powerful for you** I love the line of nature print stamps produced by Fred Mullett (listed in the Bibliography and Resources section of this book), and have used them extensively, with permission, in the Explorations in this book.
- **StazOn® stamp pads** You can certainly use other brands of stamp pads, I just love how permanent these are when dry and the fact that the ink will dry on just about any surface—even plastic! Also, you don't have to worry about the ink running if you include them in a collage with Mod Podge or acrylic paints.
- **Small spray bottles**, one filled with water and one with rubbing alcohol
- **A soft rubber brayer**
- **Lumiere® paints by Jacquard®** Acrylic paints with a lot of pigment and a lot of sparkle and shine
- **Glitter glue**

- **A small box of chalk-type pastels** I recommend avoiding oil pastels if you're just starting out as they are far more challenging to work with.
- **Beads, buttons and old jewelry**
- **Scrap fabrics or old clothes**
- **Needles, thread and embroidery floss**

- **A selection of beads**
- **Jewelry findings** like jump rings, eye pins, head pins, and closures
- **A basic jewelry-making tool set**, including smooth round-nose and chain-nose pliers

- **Basic tool set**, including gripping needle nose pliers, hammer, regular and Phillips screwdrivers, wire nips, and a hand or cordless drill
- **Craft wire**, especially 20 gauge and 22 gauge
- **Baling wire**
- **A selection of small nails, brads, tacks, screws, and screw eyes**

- **Plaster bandages** Rigid Wrap® is one brand commonly found in craft stores and can be used to make masks or draped over a simple armature for sculpting.
- **Apoxie® clay** A two-part air dry clay that can be used for sculpting and for adhering awkward, heavy, or non-porous items together
- **Acrylic caulk** This can be used for texturizing found objects or other assemblage surfaces

- **A long roll of white butcher paper or brown kraft paper** Heavy wrapping paper or old wallpaper will also work. This is handy for protecting your work surface as well as for working large.
- **A variety of handmade and machine printed papers** These are available at art supply and craft stores and can pump up your collages. Many wonderful papers are sold for scrapbooking.
- **Spray paint**
- **Hole punch** A standard office type is fine
- **A camera and a way to print copies of your photos** This might be a home printer or simply a trip to your local copy shop
- **Computer with scanner and photo editing software** This can be handy, but is definitely optional
- **Canvas boards, stretched canvas, illustration board, or wood panels for sturdier painting and/or collage surfaces** Often you can purchase scraps and ends of mat board and illustration board inexpensively from a discount art store or frame shop, and some hardware stores will also sell scrap wood for very little money. Some cities also have places where old house parts are sold and recycled, and for only a few dollars, you can pick up interior doors and cabinet doors to use as surfaces for your paintings and collages.
- **Cigar boxes or old drawers** These are great as bases for shrine construction. Check out your local smoke shop for cigar boxes. Again, some cities also have places where old house parts are sold and recycled and you can pick up old drawers for a few dollars apiece.

Art materials are delicious fun—and often, the things we have lying around the house in our junk drawers or recycling bins make the most wonderful art materials!

A Note to the Packrat
(and anyone else who likes to buy things)

We know who we are. We're the ones who bought this book, took it home, and put it on top of the stack of a dozen other books on creativity or spiritual growth or self-improvement that we've been meaning to read. We're the ones who get giddy at the thought of buying a box of new colored pencils, and then ignore that nagging feeling that we already have some somewhere. After all, the new ones will be better! You've got a box of your mom's National Geographic magazines in the basement. I've been saving a dusty box of broken china in the garage, just in case; I'm the one who got my friends to lug them out of the garage of the last place I lived when it was time to move. Four years ago.

I recognize you because it's like looking in a mirror.

And I'm bringing it up because I know from personal experience that this love of stuff can get in the way.

You already know that my studio is the size of a two-car garage. What I haven't mentioned is that it is absolutely full of stuff. I love to explore with different media, and I enjoy the hunt for new and interesting materials, and it shows. I work hard to regularly clean out the supplies, and sell or donate what I'm not using. And I work hard to actually use what is in the studio. I'm not always successful, as that box of broken china proves.

The key issue, though, is how that stuff gets there in the first place. It is glorious to wander the aisles of the art supply store, seduced by the colors or the potential uses of a new product, and then to go up to the register and buy that possibility. It is fun to get caught up in the imagination game of "what might I do with this?" in the junk store and end up at home with a bag full of pretty buttons and old bottles.

What I have realized is that I will often resort to buying things as an easy substitute for having an actual creative experience. I will get caught up in preparing to make art, or thinking about what the finished piece will look like when I do make art, or imagining how my art might look better if only I had this thing...and I will manage to spend a day shopping and then organizing and putting away my new things instead of spending a day actually in the studio making art. And I have realized that the satisfaction I get from the purchase doesn't last nearly as long as the satisfaction I get from making.

The game of possibility is a wonderful thing. And if you are a packrat like me, I encourage you to look around at what you already have and see the possibilities there. Yes, you will need some basic supplies. And, the truth is, you can make art with very little. Sharp scissors, a glue stick, and a few old magazines and junk mail can —and have—kept me creatively engaged for weeks on end. I'm going to suggest that once you've got the basic materials, you try doing some of the Artful Explorations without buying anything else...and see what happens.

Another challenge of the packrat is that the things we collect become precious. Part of why I bring a lot of supplies to the classes I teach is that I want people to experience a feeling of abundance, a feeling that they can make mistakes without using up all of their resources.

I was working with a woman in a shrine-making class, and she looked up from her work on an old drawer and said, "My old doll parts would be perfect in this!" "Great," I said, "Go for it! How do you want to attach them?" And she said, "Oh no, I don't want to actually use them—this piece is so big it would take all of them that I have, so I'm trying to think of something else."

There was a lot going on for her in the piece, including the challenge of working large. I remember thinking that from my perspective, she had the perfect number of old doll parts—enough to fill the piece. From her perspective, using all of the doll parts now would leave her without any possibilities for the future; she'd be using them all up on a piece that she was uncomfortable with anyway.

We talked about what might happen if she used the doll parts as well as what might happen if she didn't. Ultimately, it just didn't feel like a good risk for her. And I completely understood her dilemma—and her choice. In prepping for my classes, I err on the side of bringing too much stuff because I understand the fear of scarcity all too well.

You see, there were things I hadn't brought for the class to use precisely because I was saving them for some imagined future project. Some of those things have since been used in my projects, and some of them have found their way into the student bins. I too have slowly learned to trust that I can use the precious things and that if it doesn't work out, either something new (and possibly better) will come into my life or I can take the piece apart and put that perfect item aside to reuse later.

So I encourage you to go ahead. Find the old pack of colored pencils. Break open the beautiful blank journal you've been saving for something special. Haul up that box of National Geographic from the basement. Now's the time.

Materials Play Date

Materials

- Art materials you've never used
- Blank paper or sketchbook

Chances are good that you have some art materials that you've never used: a calligraphy set that you got as a gift, a set of pastels that you got on sale, or maybe even the supplies you bought when you got this book. Now is the time to pull them out and begin to experiment.

It doesn't matter if you don't know how to use them: You can learn. You can open the box and see what kinds of marks they make on the paper. You can read the instructions on the package. You can search for beginner tips online. You can test out these suggestions and see what happens. And you can let go of the need to be perfect with the materials in order to use them.

When it comes to these new materials, you are a novice. What would your expectations be of someone who had never seen, let alone used, these art materials before? Let your expectations of yourself be equally modest. What would you expect from a small child who had never used any art materials before? A mess? Wastefulness? Joyful exploration? Yes! Let yourself be that child and fill at least two sheets of paper with waste, mess, joy, and all. Here are some of my own scribbles with pastels.

TAKING IT FURTHER

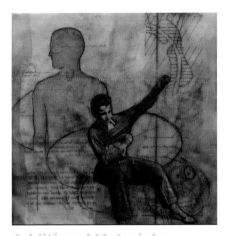

Additional Materials

- Art materials you use most often

Take those two pages of messy experimentation and consider how you might transform or use those pages now that you have your most frequently used art materials at hand. I have found that trying new things often gives me fresh insight into the familiar.

Can you take what you learned with the new materials and apply it to the familiar materials? Can you use the new materials to accent something done with your familiar materials? Can you incorporate the messy pages into another project done with your familiar materials?

For example, collage and acrylic painting might be your two most familiar mediums. You might try using the experiments with new media as a background for a painting or might cut them up and use them in a collage. A page of experimental scribbling doesn't always make its way directly into a new painting, but the experience invariably informs your future work in some way. Here is an encaustic collage where I used pastels to good effect.

Make Your Own Coloring Book

Materials

- Photocopies of your favorite images (high contrast, enlarged to about 8.5" × 11")
- Black permanent marker
- Gesso
- Small round brush
- Acrylic paints, tempera paints, or gouache

Novices often start their creative careers by copying the work of the masters; children often start with coloring books. Either way, don't be afraid to go back to the basics with some good old-fashioned tracing and copying!

1. To begin this exploration in being a novice, find some photographs or images you like. They can be from magazine ads, art books, or even photos you've taken on vacation. Generally, images with simple bold shapes and high contrast work best to start. Take the images to a copy shop and make copies of the pictures, enlarging them so they fill at least an 8.5" × 11" sheet of paper. If you can, increase the contrast so that the outlines of the images become more obvious. You can also make your copies at home using a scanner and a home printer.

2. Select one image to start. Go over the major outlines of the image with a thick black marker. This is almost like making a drawing over the copy. Don't worry about capturing detail: Just go over the lines that are essential to the image.

3. Then, fill in the outlines you've made with white gesso. Use the gesso to white out all the detail of the image, leaving just the black outline drawing. What's left is a kind of coloring book version of the original image.

4. Give the gesso half an hour or so to dry, and then begin filling in the shapes with color of your own choosing—acrylic paint works particularly well for this, though gouache also works well. See how you are echoing the image that existed before, while making it uniquely your own.

Super Simple Materials

- Original image
- Copy paper
- Sunlit window
- Blue painter's tape (or any other kind of tape you happen to have)
- Pen
- Your favorite coloring tools (like crayons or colored pencils)

Take a favorite image and tape it to a window that gets lots of light. Tape a piece of copy paper over the photo. Using a pen or pencil, trace the major outlines of the image, which should be visible thanks to the light shining through the window. (If you're not able to see it clearly, then getting a high-contrast copy of the image may help.)

Then, take the image and the tracing you made down from the window and put the original image away. Now, start coloring in your image just like a coloring book page!

Additional Materials

- Computer
- Adobe Photoshop® (or similar photo editing software)
- Printer

A. You can turn your own photos into coloring book pages using your own photo editing software like Adobe Photoshop Elements or online photo sharing sites. If you have a computer and software, follow the four simple steps in this tutorial:http://content.photojojo.com/diy/how-to-create-coloring-book-using-photos/or find a similar tutorial online by entering "make your photos into coloring pages" into your web browser.

B. If you have a computer and a printer but no gesso or photo editing software, you can also use your browser and enter a search for "adult coloring pages." Many sites offer complex and detailed coloring pages designed for adults that can be downloaded and printed out for free (and most of them are G-Rated).

For guaranteed G-Rated images, you can start here: http://adult-coloring-pages.blogspot.com/ Or get a coloring book like Monique Mandali's series of mandala coloring books, available at http://www.mandali.com

Chapter 5
Flow Factors: Creativity and the Process of ArtMaking

What Is Flow?

Moments of resistance and flow can happen at any point in the process of making art. Flow is the state of momentum we are looking to cultivate in our artmaking; Resistance is the friction that keeps us stuck. Flow happens when we are deeply connected, and it can feel as though we are in alignment with Divine purpose or the movement of the Universe. It is that place in our artmaking where we move from a monolog of self-expression into a dialog with the work itself, and time drops away. In flow, we can, if only for a few brief moments, feel like a channel for something larger than ourselves.

This doesn't mean that the self-expression, the dialog, and the channeling of artmaking are separate, or that they only occur one after the other in a distinct progression. Self-expression is usually where we start because it's what we know best. Bringing in dialog also brings in a component of conversation, of prayer. Flow is that sense of momentum and connection to Spirit. You can move back and forth through all these ways of artmaking in a matter of minutes, and they can all happen while you're working on the same piece. And we can experience the intense engagement of flow in any of these phases.

Mihayli Csikszentmihalyi has done extensive study of the flow state and what it takes to achieve it. He has found that it is most likely to occur when people are involved in challenging activities that push the limits of their ability. These activities require mindful attention, make use of their full skillset, and frequently require or engage intuitive thought. People in a flow state describe losing track of time, feeling exhilarated, and experiencing an almost effortless stream of ideas and insights. Some of the people he studied consider this to be the result of their passion and practice in their chosen field while others describe the experience as a spiritual connection. What the people he studied had in common was the fact that they were all engaged in creative problem-solving activities when they experienced flow states.

What Is Creativity?

People tend to think of creativity as a mysterious talent given to a gifted few. I find it much more valuable to think of creativity as an attitude of possibility and a process of making meaningful, useful, and novel outcomes. If creativity is an attitude, it can be developed; if it is a process, it is skill-based and can be learned. Being in flow is about being engaged in the mindful, intuitive process and attitude of creativity. When we're doing artmaking as playful prayer, we're looking to cultivate this state of creative flow.

Definition

Flow *Noun:* The state of being un-self-consciously engaged in an activity to the point that we forget about everything else and time becomes meaningless; an optimal experience so gratifying it is done for its own sake without external reward. (aAdapted from Mihayli Csikszentmihalyi in his book Flow: *The Psychology of Optimal Experience*)

Art allows us to find ourselves and lose ourselves at the same time.

–*Thomas Merton*

The only time I feel alive is when I'm painting.

–*Vincent van Gogh*

Definition

Creativity *Noun:* The yearning for and making of meaningful connections across boundaries; the attitude of possibility; the process of making the invisible visible; the making of something meaningful and novel; a state required to find novel and useful solutions to vague and difficult challenges. Artmaking is one possible expression of creativity.

People who regularly do deeply creative, engaging, and challenging tasks that require them to be mindfully in the present moment (such as the surgeons, musicians, scientists, and artists Czikszentmihalyi studied) manage to achieve states of creative flow without thinking about it. So, how do we do it if it's not already a habit? If we've experienced flow without quite understanding how it happened, how can we cultivate more moments like that? How can we translate our artmaking activities into opportunities for spiritual connection?

Components in the Practice and Process of Creative Flow

If we're thinking of creativity as a process, flow as a state we're looking to cultivate, and artmaking as prayerful dialog, then we need a practice to support it. My own practice of Creative Flow has five main components:

- GETTING CLEAR: INTENTION This is where we stand firmly in the present and come to understand and mindfully set our intentions.
- GETTING INSPIRED: ENERGY This is where we do the hard work of inspiration: exploration, experimentation, and play.
- GETTING ENGAGED: ACTION This is where we really commit, embrace the challenge, and see our project through to completion, even when it's difficult.
- STAYING IN TOUCH: INTUITION This is the center, and this is where the Source rests. This is the touchstone of values and vision. This is where we listen to our own deep knowing.
- GIVING BACK: COMMUNITY This is where community comes into our play and our prayer. This is where we ask how we can be of service and recognize what we have to offer.

The five components of the practice come together to outline a process for creativity and provide a support for ongoing work in artmaking as playful prayer. In turn, the components in this practice can serve as a kind of container for the attitudes and actions that are the work of art. You may find yourself applying these attitudes and actions in one, several, or all stages of your creative process.

Explore
Focus on Process, Not Product
Defer Judgment
Be like a Novice
Be in Conversation
Be Mindful
Follow the Energy
Let Go of the Outcome
Be Curious
Tune up Your Inner Ears
Cultivate Appreciation and Gratitude
Hold Clear Intentions

As you've probably noticed, each chapter's Artful Explorations are dedicated to one of the attitudes and actions that make up the work of art. Similarly, I've dedicated a chapter to each of the components of the practice of Creative Flow: Getting Clear, Getting Inspired, Getting Engaged, Staying in Touch, and Giving Back. As you explore them, you may find that the components become steps for you, a cycle that you move through over several months, or with the start of each new art project. Or you may find that the principles of the practice build on one another, creating a firm foundation. As you begin to work with the practice more, you may find that you move rapidly back and forth between two steps in the cycle, then leap forward, then back again before moving forward once again.

My experience has been that I dance through them, moving rapidly through the components and back in no particular order as I create, and incorporating all of the elements of Creative Flow in my daily life. Certainly, some of these elements will resonate with you more than others. I have found, though, that if I leave one component of the practice unattended for very long, I begin to feel out of balance.

On a practical level, I've found that the components of this practice do fit nicely as stages in the creative process—and correspond very closely to the stages of the well-researched processes for creative problem solving developed by Alex Osborn and Sidney Parnes (see APPENDIX A: A NOTE ON THEORY AND PRACTICE for more information). Students in my workshops who are really engaged in their artmaking are spending time on every component of the practice, every stage of the cycle, even if only for a moment. Similarly, when people are struggling or feeling uninterested, they're usually missing, skipping, or struggling with at least one piece of the process. The order, intensity, and duration of the stages in the process may vary greatly. From experience with my students, the components in the cycle are universal; however, the way they unfold as we work is unique and personal.

As I have developed and worked with the components of Creative Flow in this practice, they have come to describe not only how I do my spiritual work and my art, but they have also come to describe how I want to live my life: with clarity, inspiration, engagement, and giving, while staying firmly in touch with my values.

For me, this practice has the potential to engage the whole person in a spiritual way. It's not simply about flow, it's also about bringing creativity and spirituality into every part of our lives. It's the foundation for artmaking as playful prayer.

Strong and convincing art has never risen from theories.

–Mary Wigman

A Note about Following Processes You Read about in Books

Every now and then, you'll need to break the rules. What I've described here is an intuitive process that I've experienced, observed, and researched—I've just given it a fancy name and hopefully made it easy to understand. However, I am not a guru and none of what I describe is carved in stone. My hope is that it will help you break through some blocks and discover some things about your own creative process. And it is also my hope that you will take what is useful to you and ignore the rest. Listen to yourself. The greatest teacher you will ever know is in there.

We learn by practice. Whether it means to learn to dance by practicing dancing or to learn to live by practicing living, the principles are the same. One becomes in some area an athlete of God.

–Martha Graham

Artful Explorations: Be in Conversation

Talk with the Book

Materials
- This book
- Pen
- Permanent black marker
- Junk mail or old magazines
- Other collage materials
- Glue stick
- Scissors
- Your favorite drawing or coloring materials

Begin a conversation with this book. It's your book. Underline passages that speak to you. Make comments in the margins. Circle things. Cross things out. Highlight topics in the index. Try different kinds of pens. Find one that marks well on the paper without smearing or one that smears in an appealing way. Respond to what's in the book.

Use color and images to add to the conversation. Use markers, crayons, or colored pencils to highlight headlines. Add to the artwork in this book by pumping up the color or doodling along the edges. Collage into the book, pasting found images, words, or quotes where they most need to be added.

Make this book your own.

TAKING IT FURTHER

Additional Materials
- Blank paper or sketchbook (larger is better)
- Gesso
- Mod Podge or acrylic medium
- Acrylic paints
- Brushes and water container

OPTIONAL
- Wax paper or palette

If you can't quite imagine yourself marking up a book—or if you find yourself wanting to add so much to the book that it becomes illegible—take heart! Make photocopies of your favorite pages in the book and use Mod Podge or acrylic medium to paste the copies into the pages of a sketchbook. Use this as the beginning point for an interactive journaling session!

Artful Explorations: Be in Conversation

Talk with Your Space

Materials

- The stuff that's in your house
- Journal or notepad
- Pen or pencil

1. Begin by leaving your home with paper and pencil in hand. Stand outside and take a few deep breaths. Imagine that you are a visitor, perhaps an anthropologist studying a foreign culture, and that you have never visited this house before.

2. Now, enter the house as a visitor would. For example, if you normally come in through the garage, but a visitor would come to the front door, enter through the front door.

3. Look (with fresh eyes) at the first room you see. What is the predominant theme, color, or texture in the room? What seems to be the focus of the space? What's on display and what's hidden? What is there a lot of? What's missing? What's the biggest object or mass of objects in the room? Make notes about what you see.

4. Now, wander from room to room. Poke in closets and medicine cabinets like a noscy stranger. Based only on what you observe, ask yourself, "What's important to the person or people who live here?" Make notes on your notepad. Come up with at least 16 things that are important to this family based on what you've observed.

5. Then, consider what you observed. Did anything surprise you? How closely do the things on the list match what you really think is important?

One of the things that I noticed about my own home when I did this was the overwhelming number of pillows I have. They are everywhere. You almost can't sit down for all the pillows. I'd never really thought about it before, but I love textiles and I love comfort. The pillows are all about cozy, cushy, pretty comfort for me. They make me feel pampered and surrounded by soft beauty, like some lovely woman in a colorful painting by Matisse, even when the sheer volume of them seems to get in the way.

Until I did this, I hadn't realized how important feeling comfortable and surrounded by beauty was to me. It's amazing what we hear when we stop and listen.

A. Did you notice any shrine-like areas in your house, areas where emotionally or spiritually significant objects are gathered or displayed? It may have been created consciously or may have happened unconsciously. It can be as simple as a collection of family photos on the mantle, a cluster of travel postcards on the fridge, or a set of Star Trek figurines on your computer. Often, these spaces offer subtle (and not-so-subtle) communications to us about what's really important in our lives.

If the shrine-like spaces are conscious, take some time now to clean and refresh them. Update the family photos, dust the frames, freshen the nearby flower arrangement. If the shrine-like area is unconscious, think about what it would look like if you were intentionally creating a space to honor your love of travel or vintage science fiction memorabilia. Would you dedicate a shelf to it? Set aside a special bulletin board? What might you include that's not already there?

B. If you didn't notice any shrine-like spaces in your home or found that your home didn't really reflect what was important to you, consider establishing a space where significant objects can gather. If your home is largely the product of the tastes of a spouse or housemate, is there a space you can claim for your own? Think about what part of your history, dreams, or passions you want to acknowledge or honor. What objects in your home are representative of that? Is there a place where they can come together for added impact?

C. Similarly, consider what you might need to get rid of or let go of. Is your house full of furniture that you inherited from your great aunt but don't really like? Do you still have posters on the wall from bands you quit listening to ten years ago? Did you somehow acquire an elephant collection that really isn't important anymore?

Part of exercising our creative muscles and being in conversation is to pause, deeply notice, and listen to what's going on around us. Engaging your surroundings in conversation is good practice for learning to listen to your art.

Chapter 6
Getting Clear: Intention

The Value of Intention

There are a lot of ways to think about this first step in the process, and a lot of clearing to do around artmaking and creative process. Yet I find again and again in artmaking that the most important thing to get clear about is my intentions.

Somewhere along my own path back to joyful artmaking, I began to realize that every time I sat down to make art, there was a lot more to it. As I said earlier, making art, at that point in my life, meant making something really, really impressive that potential art collectors and imaginary gallery owners and future museum curators and my many non-existent lovers would like. Every time I sat down alone to make art, my real intention was to win praise from people I'd never met.

It meant that I couldn't make things that were ugly or bad. It meant that I couldn't make mistakes. No wonder I wasn't that interested in making art anymore. It was so much about the product—and so much about other people—that there was no room for me to be a human being engaged in the act of making.

As you can guess, I didn't make a lot of art during this time in my life.

> **Definition**
>
> **Intention** *Noun:* The underlying plan, goal, resolve, or focus that consciously or subconsciously guides a series of actions; an attitude that shapes perceptions, actions, and outcomes; the object for which a prayer, mass, or pious act is offered. Plural: purpose with respect to a deeper commitment or marriage (as in "What are your intentions?")

Setting Intention, Setting Attitude

Now, I try to consciously set my artmaking intentions. My intention sets my attitude: The intention sets the way I will be working that day and guides my decision-making. I set my intention before I start working, beginning with "I will" or "I am." It might be as focused as "I will stay present in the moment and keep my inner ears open" or as simple as "I am here to explore and have fun today." Sometimes I forget and will need to pause during the middle of an artmaking session to remind myself why I'm really there!

I am careful to set intentions that are centered on the attitudes, actions, or processes of artmaking—not on outcomes or final products. Flow is found in the doing. When I am engaged in artmaking as playful prayer, I am not envisioning the final product. I might say, "I will be very attentive in my artmaking today and deeply notice what I am drawing" rather than "I will make a very detailed and accurate drawing." The object I am making is not the goal; the attitude with which I approach the making is the goal.

Beware, too, of setting intentions like "I will have a spiritual experience" or "I am going to connect with the Divine." No one works well under that kind of pressure. Instead, consider setting an intention like "I will be open to Divine connection" or "I am open to whatever Spirit has to offer today." Again, focus your intentions on actions and attitudes, not specific outcomes.

Arranging your space with some kind of spiritual signifier, as I discussed earlier, can help reinforce your ongoing intentions—especially in those moments when you forget to set an intention. A laughing Buddha may help remind you to have fun or a collection of stones may remind you stay present and grounded in the moment. In many of my classes, I ask students to blindly select a small touchstone with a word or image carved in it. It is amazing how often each student receives exactly what they need: Words like "joy," "peace," "insight," or the simple image of an angel or the Buddha can help students stay in touch with their deeper purpose.

Of course, my own hidden agenda of making brilliant art that critics will swoon over does bubble up. My job is simply to notice that impulse, and to continue to act upon my original, consciously set intention. And that's the challenge. Those other desires, the old attitudes, the habitual patterns, they don't go away. They still come up. The question is this: Can we acknowledge that hidden agenda and make the conscious choice to take different actions?

> ## A Conversation with Your Intentions
>
> To uncover your own hidden artmaking agendas and consciously set new ones that will better support the goal of artmaking as playful prayer, I encourage you to do some conversational journaling with your intentions. Ask some questions on paper and see what you have to say as you let the answers come out through your pen. Don't judge or edit the answers that appear; just write the first things that pop into your head.
>
> - When I make art, what am I really hoping will happen?
> - When I make art, what am I expecting will happen?
> - What are my secret fantasies about myself as an artist?
> - What's the worst thing that will happen if my hopes, expectations, and fantasies don't come true?
> - What other intentions might I hold when I make art? What might be the results?
>
> As I said earlier, spiritual work is a constant dance of will and surrender, and artmaking is no different from any other path in that regard. Setting the intention is the act of your will; being in a place of mindfulness is an act of surrender.

Clearing Your Mind

One of the great challenges in any kind of meditation or intentional focus is that our minds are really busy and very easily distracted. Some of you may have already worked to develop a meditation practice, and for those of you who have, I recommend taking a few moments to meditate before starting an artmaking session; it will put you into a frame of mind where you can notice the chatter and not be driven by it. In my artmaking as playful prayer classes, I have found that taking a few moments to gather everyone together and do a guided visualization or set a few meaningful items on an art room altar helps set the tone and intention for the session.

If you're like me—and a lot of other Westerners—you may be intimidated by traditional sitting meditation. The thought of sitting quietly and doing nothing just about sends me into a panic. Yoga and journaling have proven more effective mind-clearing activities for me. Part of why I like artmaking as a prayerful, meditative act is that it is a moving meditation. I even enjoy some of the more mundane and repetitive actions of artmaking—drilling holes in 500 plastic bottle caps for a sculpture or priming 20 canvases.

Definition

Mindfulness *Noun:* A state of being where we are actively present in the moment, aware of and not attached to experiences and outcomes; a fluid, responsive, grounded state of awareness; being aware of mental activity while simultaneously being detached from it.

The simple activity actually helps me be more mindful and pulls me more solidly into the present moment. It gives my magpie brain something to focus on so that my Inner Self has space to be heard.

Part of Getting Clear is learning to set aside or ignore our mental clutter so that Spirit has room to speak. With practice, it has become much easier for me to set a simple intention, step into my studio, and be absolutely in the moment, making, listening, responding.

Of course, it doesn't work that way all the time. You may find, like I sometimes do, that you aren't in the moment, that you don't actually hear the Inner Self. Instead, you may find that the Inner To-Do List, the Inner Critic, or the Inner Worry Wart takes the opportunity to pipe up and fill the void.

When this happens, there are a number of things that you can do to cultivate a state of mindfulness. You can take the mental clutter and clear it, ground it, or engage it. Any of these can help you set the clutter aside and be more in the moment.

CLEAR IT

One reason why so many people swear by Julia Cameron's morning pages, the 3-page written stream-of-consciousness brain dump suggested in her book *The Artist's Way*, is that it is such an effective mental clutter-clearing tool. Morning pages, journaling, jotting down notes, making lists: Any of these can help. The pen acts almost like a drain, letting all the distracting stuff run out of your head and onto the page. The process of writing can also help you identify root issues and understand what's really going on. Try doing some kind of writing either before you start your artmaking or as part of your everyday routine. It can help you flush out the mental waste and stay "regular."

If you're not comfortable writing, you can try talking into a tape recorder or making sure that you talk with a friend or loved one every day about the "little stuff" that's going on. If there's more going on than a friend can easily handle, sharing with a therapist or counselor on a consistent basis may also help you clear a little space.

GROUND IT

A sensitive and powerful appliance, or a piece of equipment that runs a lot of current, will have three prongs on its plug instead of two. While the reason is a bit convoluted to a non-electrician like me, the bottom line is that the extra prong helps to ground the appliance, protecting the appliance and the user from electricity gone haywire. People are sensitive and powerful equipment. We run a lot of energy, and we need to be grounded. Most of us ground through our bodies—it's the extra prong at the end of our mental-emotional-spiritual power cord.

And yet how many of us ignore our bodies? Try doing some yoga, stretching, or even taking a 20-minute walk before you go into an artmaking session. Try dancing all out to a favorite song or doing a guided meditation that gets you firmly in your body and connects you back to the earth. If you do, you will be more present in your physical self, and more in the moment, and thus more mindful. You may also find that your chattering mind takes a back seat for a while.

ENGAGE IT

Just like our physical clutter, our mental clutter can be made up of things we are avoiding that need our attention. The stack of unpaid bills on the dining room table?

THE CREATIVE CONVERSATION: ARTMAKING AS PLAYFUL PRAYER

The broken chair shoved in a corner of your office? The unanswered emails in the inbox? All of these physical and digital manifestations of clutter have mental counterparts: the nagging financial worry, the disturbing unsettled issue at work, the lingering misunderstanding with a friend. Just like you have to take action to clear the physical clutter, sometimes you have to fully engage to clear the mental clutter.

Artmaking is a great opportunity to engage. Instead of trying to tune out the chatter while you work, try tuning in more fully. Use your artmaking as a chance to explore what's going on in your head. If you're worried about a lingering misunderstanding with a friend, what does it feel like? And what does that feeling look like? What shape is it? What color is it? What animal is it like? Start painting or drawing!

Go with your first impulses—don't worry about whether it "fits" with the image or the painting. Don't worry whether you can draw at all. Just draw the jagged brown lines or the orange leopard and her big fangs or the lime green bumblebee with the twitchy eyes. What's the next impulse? Does the brown jagged line turn into mountains and lighting? Is the leopard in a boat? Does the bumblebee have an umbrella? Scribble, scrawl, dive in and don't analyze. And then you may find that you feel more clear and connected. So draw what that feels like. And so on.

Getting Clear outside of Your Head: Your Space

While mindfulness and clear intentions are important parts of being clear, there are other components of Getting Clear that happen outside your head.

Clearing your space is one piece of that equation, and part of why I spent time in this book up front talking about making a space for making. If that space gets too cluttered (and only you will know what "too cluttered" means for you), then working in that space will become more difficult. Some people need to have everything in labeled bins and a large clear work surface before they can even think of starting; others only feel a clog in the creative flow when the heaps of unfinished projects and half-used art materials make it difficult to open the door.

I have one friend who will get rid of things if they don't work for her after a couple of tries, or if she feels her work has moved in a different direction. She seems to have a studio clearing sale at least once a year, and there isn't much room for "I might use that someday" stuff in her life. I read about another artist who finally decided she needed to clear out and clean her studio only when she realized she had been avoiding the space for several months.

My clutter-clearing moment is somewhere in the middle. When it starts to get difficult to find my favorite tools, or I discover a half-finished project that no longer interests me, or I notice a bin of materials set aside and untouched for a year, that's a signal to me that it's time to clear some space. And an interesting thing happens—I feel more focused and energized when I've let go of things that are no longer serving me. If you're interested in learning more about the energetic impact of clutter, I recommend the book *Clear Your Clutter with Feng Shui* by Karen Kingston.

You are lost the instant you know what the result will be.

–Juan Gris

A work of art is above all an adventure of the mind.

–Eugene Ionesco

Definition

Clear *Adjective:* Without distortion or obstruction; empty; pure; without blemish.

Deep Observation Drawing

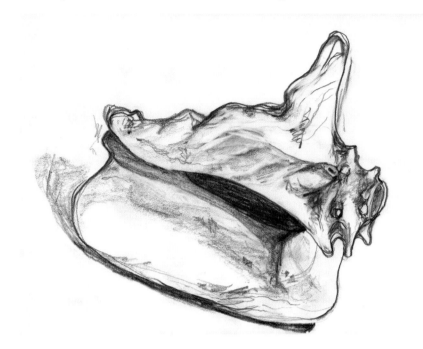

Materials

- Your favorite drawing tools
- An everyday object
- Blank paper or sketchbook

1. To begin, find an object in your home to draw. It may be best if it's something you use every day and take for granted, though it might also be something with compelling shapes, textures, contrasts, or lines. I suggest beginning with something that seems simple: Trust me, anything that we pay close attention to and then try to draw will grow in complexity as the process unfolds.

2. Get into a comfortable position with the object in view and your drawing materials at hand. Now, take a few moments and really look at it. Use your eyes to appreciate the object. What is the basic shape of it? What are the textures? Are there flaws or perfections about it you had never noticed before? What is your emotional response?

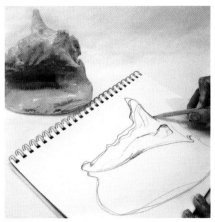

3. Now, begin to record your observation by drawing. Use your drawing tool to record that particular swooping line or that rigid shape. Avoid using color at first. If it's not quite right, don't erase: Just draw another observation on top of that one. Let your marks be varied and reflect the surfaces you are recording—soft, hard, thick, thin, jagged, smooth.

4. As with the Blind Drawing we did earlier, it is important to remember that you are not making a reproduction of the object. You are making a record of your observation and interaction with this object. Your drawing will be influenced by your mood, your experience of the object, your skill. Some elements may be represented as larger than they are in reality, while others may be smaller. You may choose to emphasize certain things that fascinate you or make them larger to get at the detail.

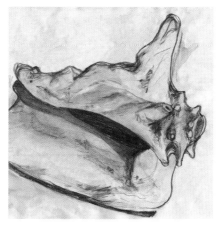

5. If you use an eraser, use it as a drawing tool rather than a correction tool. Use an eraser when you need to emphasize a highlight or sharpen a line.

6. Keep noticing and recording, building up layers of marks and shading, until everything you've visually experienced about the object (with the exception of color) is reflected in the marks on the page.

Additional Materials A

• Your favorite painting or coloring materials

A. Now, try doing the same thing, only this time, use color! Try adding paints, crayons, or colored pencils into the mix.

Additional Materials B

• Mirror

B. Turn the same deeply appreciative gaze on yourself. Your own face is certainly a surface you know well, but you probably don't spend a great deal of time appreciating it. Try approaching a self-portrait as a record of your observation and interaction, and see what happens.

Dancing with Matisse: Color Cuts

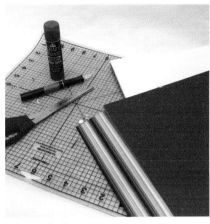

Materials

- Blank paper or sketchbook
- Glue stick
- Colored construction paper or origami paper
- Scissors and/or craft knife

OPTIONAL

- Camera or phone with camera

Towards the end of his career, French painter Henri Matisse began working with cut paper. He had always been interested in line and color, and by working directly with colored paper, he was able to use scissors as his drawing implement. He worked large, and some of the pieces were designs for stained glass windows.

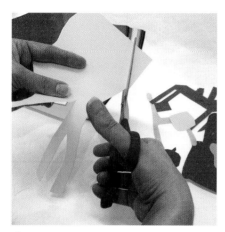 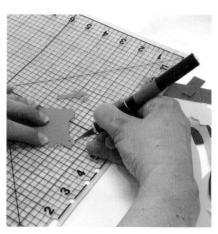 

1. Gather your paper and begin cutting out shapes. The only rules: Cut without drawing on the paper first, don't use a ruler, and don't rip or tear the paper to shape it. Always use your scissors or your craft knife to draw the line.

The shapes can be abstract or representative. You may want to draw on nature, as Matisse frequently did, for inspiration, looking to the softly rounded shapes of corals and leaves.

You may be drawn to human forms like strong calves or open hands. You may want to work with large fields of color like squares or circles. You may find it interesting to cut out shapes that are reminiscent of household objects like chairs, fruits, or bowls.

2. Make small shapes and large shapes. Use lots of different colors, and cut out more than you think you might ever use. Cut at least 20 shapes before you begin to arrange them.

3. Once you have 20–30 cut-paper shapes, begin arranging them on a piece of sketch paper. You might choose to leave lots of white space, like Matisse often did, or you may choose to fill the space with color. You may use all your shapes, or only 3. You may find that you want to cut more shapes or that a certain arrangement needs another shape. Go ahead and cut it.

Additional Materials

• Large paper (like a roll of butcher or craft paper)

Get a large piece of paper, like a roll of craft paper or butcher paper, and use this same process to design a stained glass window. What might be the theme? What might be the background colors? What might the glass shapes look like?

4. Allow yourself time to try different combinations and arrangements of color. If you discover a composition you really like while you are exploring, try taking a quick snapshot of it with your camera or even your phone, then continue exploring.

5. Now, begin gluing down your arrangements. You may have only one arrangement, or you may have several. You can always reference your snapshots if you need to remember exactly how your favorite compositions looked.

Chapter 7
Getting Inspired: Energy

The Myth and Reality of Inspiration

There are a lot of myths about inspiration. Perhaps the most insidious of them is the idea that artists sit around and wait for inspiration to strike, only proceeding in their work when they are in the right mood and "moved by the muse." Here's the truth. Inspiration doesn't lead to work; work leads to inspiration. We have to be actively doing the work of art in order to find inspiration—or for inspiration to find us.

The words inspiration, perspiration, and spirit share the same root, which means "breath." Inspiration, like breath and the Divine, requires that we open up and let it in. And, as perspiration implies, we've got to work for it. As artists, we can't expect inspiration to show up if we simply sit around ignoring our artwork and complaining about being blocked. As spiritual beings, we can't expect enlightened answers to appear to us while we sit around whining about how horrible our life is.

In artmaking as playful prayer, inspiration is active, not passive. We get inspired; we find things inspiring. This means that you can let go of the notion of needing to "be inspired" to make art. In fact, to get in the mood, to consistently be in the mood, you need to consistently do the work. In order for inspiration to be a regular occurrence, artmaking—and the work of art—needs to become a practice, a discipline, and finally a habit.

The good news is that the hard work of inspiration is actually a lot of fun—and can become as automatic as breathing.

> **Definition**
>
> **Inspiration** *Noun:* Divine guidance or influence; the act of breathing; stimulation to a high level of function or feeling; a moment of insight during which a previously unseen connection is recognized; an ongoing series of insights and realizations that keep us in creative motion; the fuel of flow.

Let It Happen by Doing It

One of the things I see consistently in my classes is that students don't want to start working because they "don't have an idea yet." This is part of why this book gives you lots of possible projects to use as starting points. You don't have to have it all figured out before you start; you simply need a general direction. Our goal with artmaking as a spiritual practice is not to rapidly and efficiently reach our final destination; it is to journey in such a way that we listen, learn, and grow.

Just as the thought "I'm interested in exploring" and the fact that you have only your feet and $1.23 for transport can effectively guide a day's wanderings, your artmaking intention and your available materials will provide you with a basic direction in your artmaking. Let where you are and what you have serve as your starting point, and let your intention be your compass. Exploration doesn't require a map; exploration creates one.

In my classes, I provide as many of the materials as possible, and try to reinforce learning, playing, and exploring as the key intentions. I encourage people to explore the materials, to gather the paints or papers or beads or colors that attract their attention. I encourage students to begin playing with arranging the papers they've

> *The only way to do it is to do it.*
>
> –Merce Cunningham

> *Inspiration exists, but it has to find you working.*
>
> –Pablo Picasso

collected, making marks on the paper, or using the paints to try out different color combinations. Invariably, the students will discover some color, image, or object that excites them. Something will spark a connection, and they will begin to see a number of possible directions they could move in. By beginning to work, they find inspiration.

Let It Happen by Letting It Go

Perhaps the second most insidious inspiration myth is the idea that inspiration always comes in one giant bang, giving us a fully-formed Idea that we then go forth and implement exactly as it has appeared in our heads. Generally, inspiration is more subtle and more incremental. Yes, the big bangs happen, and for every huge Idea, there are a hundred smaller insights, little sparks that light the way forward and keep the momentum going. As a result of the ongoing process of inspiration, the big Ideas change and grow. And they beget other Ideas.

The days you work are the best days.

–Georgia O'Keefe

For every student who comes into class with no inspiration, there is one who shows up with an Idea. These students have already gone from Intention to fully implemented Product in their heads and are looking to use the class time to Make It Real. They may hang onto their Idea like a life raft, keeping a firm grip no matter how the sea below them teems with new inspirations and currents pulling them in new directions. Sometimes, people are afraid that someone else will steal their Idea, or they're afraid that they won't be able to implement the Idea well. Unfortunately, in each case, they usually end up dissatisfied, having cheated themselves out of the joy of the process. To echo St. Francis of Assisi, a craftsman will use his hands and his head to create something, applying incredible skill to recreate exactly what appeared in her head. The artist, however, is also letting her heart get involved; the artist is engaging Spirit. The artist is involved in a dialog, and so the artist must be open to change.

Great ideas originate in the muscles.

–Thomas Edison

Remember that artmaking as a spiritual practice is a moving meditation; part of the value lies in the physical process of making. It's fine if you have an image of the finished project in your mind.

Nothing you write, if you hope to be any good, will ever come out as you first hoped.

–Lillian Hellman

And just like no child will grow into the adult you daydreamed about during your months of pregnancy, no idea will arrive on the canvas exactly the way you pictured it in your head. Let that finished product, that Idea, stay where it is. You've already done a wonderful job of building it there. Now let the idea serve as a starting point in the world of making. It can be like your materials and intentions in that it sets a direction, not the destination.

Trust me. It's not the only Idea you'll ever have.

You Can Have Lots of Ideas

Relaxing, seeing connections, and perceiving the myriad of possibilities doesn't come easily to everyone. Like any skill, they take practice.

The ability to see many different possibilities and generate lots of ideas is also called *divergent thinking*. In school, as in most of life, we are not taught to find many possible answers; we are taught to find THE right answer. If we are taught to think at all, we are taught to think critically, not divergently. Yet this ability to generate lots of ideas is considered a hallmark of the creative mind. I firmly believe that we all have the seed of this creative ability; this adaptability is part of what makes us human. We're simply not encouraged to use it or have no practice in applying it. So, for many of us, the ability never blossoms.

To build up your divergent thinking muscles and get your ideating brain in gear, try integrating more exploring, experimentation, and play into your day: I've compiled a list of possible explorations to get you started here. In *The Artist's Way*, Julia Cameron proposes taking yourself on artist's dates, which serve much the same function. And when Eric Booth talks about "the everyday work of art," he's referring to brain-stretching and imagination-building tasks just like the ones I've listed here.

- **Try watching a documentary** about something that interests you and that you've never taken the time to learn about. That film about underwater oddities may spark a whole new set of visual metaphors.
- **Take a class in something** you were always told you weren't good at and wanted to do anyway, like a martial arts group for the clumsy or improvisational jazz singing for the tone deaf. You'll learn a lot—and perhaps discover that you're not as clumsy or tone deaf as you thought.
- **Try a new food**. Buy a different brand of cereal, select an exotic fruit in the produce aisle, or try a new restaurant—maybe one featuring the cuisine of a country you've always wanted to visit. Sure, there's always the chance that you won't like it. So what? What if you do like it?
- **Be a tourist in your own life**. Consider something you do as part of your regular routine—taking the bus to work, doing laundry, driving to the grocery store. Now, really notice it, one sense at a time. One day, try noting everything you smell during that activity; another time, be aware of every sound. Devote one time to touch, another to sight. If you can, write down each thing you notice as you go through your routine. You might even try taking a camera (or a phone with a camera) with you during the activity, as suggested earlier. How does your daily life change as you deeply notice and document it?
- **Make up stories**. As you ride the bus or subway, try to imagine how that man came to be wearing mismatched socks or how those two people met. Come up with as many stories as possible, no matter how ridiculous—go for at least a dozen, more if you can.
- **Make up even more elaborate stories**. Driving to work or walking around town on errands, consider how Bob's Pawn Shop came to be, who lives in the apartment over the donut shop, or who has the job of naming all the colors at the paint store. What do they look like? How did they get started? What do they eat for breakfast? If you don't have to worry about

operating a motor vehicle as your mind wanders, try writing your thoughts down or speaking them into a tape recorder.

- **Find connections**. Try playing the "If I were a fruit, what fruit would I be and why?" game. Play it alone or with friends, and try comparing yourself and others to as many different types of objects as possible. What kind of animal, store, art supply, undergarment, country, or small electrical appliance would you or your best friend be? If every member of your family were a piece of furniture, what would they be and how would they fit into a room together?

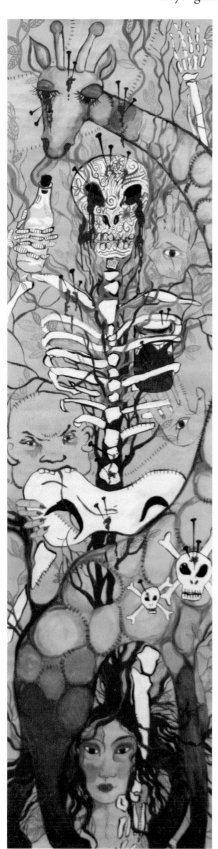

- **Take the connections game even further** and begin to think in metaphor and simile. Take two disparate objects and consider how they might be similar, or how they might be related. You can select objects from the dictionary, from a random magazine page, or from within your line of sight. How is a book of poetry like a fork? How is an onion like a park bench? Consider all the characteristics of each and consider what characteristics they might share. Sharp? Shiny? Round? Peeling? Next, take a situation and an object and consider their similarities. How is my relationship with my sister like a fork? How is my job like a park bench?

- **Play with your art materials** and get to know them. See how many different marks you can make with a pencil, or how many different colors you can get with the paints. See how many different ways the six magazine images you cut out can be combined.

- **Change your language**. Every time you find yourself complaining or worrying over a situation, try rephrasing it as a question that starts with "How might I …" or "What are all the ways I could …" For example, instead of saying to yourself, "I hate rush hour traffic!" try saying: "How might I avoid rush hour traffic?" Changing the way you consider the challenge totally changes your thinking and pushes you to come up with as many solutions as possible. So go for it—a dozen ideas is the bare minimum. After the obvious answers like "quit my job," "work 11 am to 7 pm," "telecommute," and "ride a bike to work," you might start getting to some interesting ones like "hitchhike with aliens," "only travel by helicopter," or "move to a four-star hotel near work." Even the crazy ideas that seem unreasonable in the moment may lead to a workable solution. Even if you can't hitchhike with aliens, you might be able to catch a ride with a co-worker. Hopefully, you'll get a few laughs and at the very least, it will remind you that you do have some control in the situation: You have the ability to guide your own thinking and to make different choices.

- **Cut the "but."** Try going for an entire day without using the word "but" in your written or spoken communications. Using "but" stops us. Try replacing "but" with "and" and see what happens.

At the root of all of these exercises is cultivating an attitude of possibility and getting out of the "one right answer" mindset. I remember hearing a story about the head librarian at a large metropolitan library. She was interviewing new hires, and when she was asked what she was looking for, she said, "Someone who's worked in at least three libraries. If you've worked in one library, you know the right way to do things. If you've worked in two libraries, you know the right way and the wrong way to do things. If you've worked in three libraries, you know what needs to get done, and you know several different ways to make it happen."

That Doesn't Sound like Work to Me!

"Okay," a few of you may be thinking. "She talked about inspiration being a lot of work, the whole inspiration is 90% perspiration thing. Right! Making up stories about strangers on a bus? Photographing my laundry? Eating weird foods? That's not work—that's goofing off!"

Precisely! It's play, which we defined at the very beginning as joyful, intuitive learning. It's important to take time to explore and do the things that don't immediately seem productive. The best kind of work is virtually indistinguishable from play. So, how do you know when you're engaged in the kind of relaxation and explorative play that leads to inspiration and when you're engaged in the sort of goofing off that constitutes avoidance and resistance? And when are you goofing off just because, well, it's time to goof off?

It's not easy. As human beings, we need rest. Yes, we need sleep, and we also need restful awake time. Time being active and not necessarily productive. Time spent in the today, not in the to-do.

Integration and gestation take time, quiet time, and this is where the myth of the sudden breakthrough inspiration comes from. Yes, the ideas seem to come to us miraculously in the shower, or the solution appears out of nowhere as we walk the labyrinth. It happens when our deep selves, warmed up from a simile game, relaxed from a walk in the neighborhood, and now meandering through the taste of a new food, make a connection. It may seem like it came out of the blue. The truth is, we've done the work of inspiration and given ourselves the space to have the insight.

I also believe we need goof-off time, time when we are passively entertained. Time to watch TV, nap on the beach, or read a fantasy novel. Sometimes the only thing that separates the work of inspiration from goofing off is our attitude. Are we passively napping on the beach, or are we actively experiencing the feeling of sun on our skin and the myriad of scents playing across our senses—the coconut smell of sunscreen, the tang of saltwater, the moldering of sea grasses? If you're like me, you slip back and forth between active and passive, explorative play and goofing off.

> So you see, imagination needs moodling—long, inefficient, happy idling, dawdling, and puttering.
>
> –Brenda Ueland

> ## A Conversation with Avoidance and Your Inner Goof-Off
> It can be difficult to recognize when passive goofing-off time has moved into avoidance or resistance. If all you have is a nagging feeling that you "should be doing something productive," let it go. However, if you answer yes to one or more of the following questions, there's a good chance that you're avoiding something, and that it's time to switch out of goof-off mode:

- Is the passive entertainment starting to feel compulsive or addictive? In other words, do I keep doing it even when the pleasure of the activity is fading in an attempt to satisfy a craving, soothe an ache or fill a void?
- Have I made a commitment that I will not be able to keep if I continue to engage in this activity?
- Am I feeling sluggish, lethargic, or bored?
- Is there a challenge I am capable of taking action to resolve or an important matter that I can move forward on and am avoiding? Am I avoiding taking action because of fear, guilt, or shame?
- Am I feeling overwhelmed by what I think I need to be accomplishing?

If a yes answer pops up, it may be time to take some action. It could be as simple as moving your body, breaking a task down into smaller bits, or even letting go of some of the things you think you need to be doing. It can be as simple as saying out loud to someone, "I'm really stuck on this." Sometimes, you just need to step back and get clear again on what your intentions really are.

Take a few minutes and do some conversational journaling on each of these questions, or try asking these questions aloud or in your head. What is the first thing to pop up in answer to each of these questions?

And Yes, You Can Have Too Many Ideas!

Of course, for some people, the thing that proves overwhelming is having too many

ideas! If you are so overcome with inspiration and possibilities that you can't choose a direction, have 20 projects begun and none finished, or if you get distracted in the middle of a project and have to go start something new, then the hardest part of inspiration for you is focus. This is a process, which means we don't spend all of our time in explorative play or getting inspired. We don't spend all of our time in the starting blocks, gazing down the track. Eventually, we have to commit and take off running. In one direction.

Focusing, narrowing down the options, and making choices is called convergent thinking, and it's the opposite of divergent thinking. It's also equally important. And, just like divergent thinking, it's not about finding one right answer. Convergent thinking is about finding the best solution in a given situation. Given the same options, the best idea for one situation is not necessarily the best idea for a similar situation occurring two hours later. Similarly, there may be six perfectly good ways of solving the challenge: Convergent thinking can simply help you identify the solution that best fits your skills and available resources.

So how do you choose which idea to pursue? How do you know which way to run? How do you focus? You've got to make a choice. While I go into more depth about making choices during the artmaking process in the next chapter, I want to take a few moments now to talk about making the choices that will help you get started in the artmaking process.

A Conversation with an Overload of Ideas

If you have a lot of ideas, try asking yourself these questions to determine which idea is one that you may want to pursue NOW. Again, use a conversational journaling style. Ask the question, and let your inner self answer the question through your pen.

- Am I really excited about it, or does it just seem like something I should do? Hint: Let go of the shoulds and go for the ideas that excite you. Follow the energy.
- Can I start it right now, or does it require materials or training I don't have at hand? Hint: Go for the project you can start right away. If the project requires materials you don't have, or you need to learn how to use a blow torch to complete the project, schedule a time to get the materials or training. Don't use it as an excuse to put off your artmaking.
- What intentions, expectations, and fantasies are attached to the idea? Hint: Go for the ideas that are joyful and fun, preferably ones you haven't made up a lot of stories about. Maybe try the project that you haven't spent time envisioning in the Louvre or in a place of honor in your mother's living room.
- How's the scope—how doable does the project seem? Hint: At least at first, go for projects that seem doable—or break them down into doable chunks. Challenge is inherent in the process, and you will soon discover that you are capable of far more than you thought. Challenge, however, is different from frustration and overwhelm, and there's no reason to set yourself up for a lousy time.

Do what you can with what you have where you are.

–*Theodore Roosevelt*

The most important factor is your level of energy and excitement. Just because you have the materials to do a project, have few fantasies attached to it, and it feels doable doesn't mean you have to do it—if it feels too much like a should, save it for later and go after the idea that seems the most exciting. We want artmaking to become a habit, and habits are generally built on rewards. Following the energy is part of what makes the artmaking feel good. The energy is part of what keeps the momentum going, makes artmaking something we want to keep doing, and turns artmaking into a habit.

Of course, we're just using these questions to help determine what to work on NOW. It doesn't mean that you are abandoning the other ideas. Keep a journal for all of your amazing ideas. Eventually, it will either be the perfect time to do them or they will lose their appeal.

Just Paint, Just Draw

Materials

- Blank paper or sketchbook (larger is better)
- Gouache, tempera, or acrylic paints
- Brushes and water container

OPTIONAL

- Blue painter's tape
- Wax paper or palette

1. Collect your materials and lay out your paints. Here, I prepared by laying out some colors of gouache on a wax paper palette.

2. Wet a brush—just pick the one that speaks to you—and pick up some color. Again, go with your gut and choose the first color that you're drawn to.

3. Start making a shape that feels good.

4. Repeat. If something comes into your mind, and you want to paint it, do it. I had an urge to paint a monkey, and I've never painted a monkey before. I've drawn them while looking at pictures, but never just painted one out of my head before. And I just did it. It's not the greatest looking monkey, but I know it's a monkey. And that's all that matters.

5. Keep building up shapes, adding colors and objects. Let go of whether it's pretty or looks good or makes any sense. Just follow the energy and have fun.

6. Don't obliterate or destroy anything just because you don't like it. You can layer on top of it (my final monkeys look a lot different from that first one, but they're all still in there!) while still respecting what you initially created. Sometimes, if something looks weird, the answer is just to put more of them in. And sometimes, it just needs more swirly shapes or dots or colors.

7. Keep going until there's nothing else you want to put in. We'll talk more about completion in the next chapter, but for now, just keep going until you've tried everything you wanted to try.

SUPER SIMPLE OPTION

Super Simple Materials
- Your favorite drawing tools

1. Pick up your pen or pencil and start doodling on the page. Make shapes or patterns that feel good.

2. If something comes into your mind, and you want to draw it, draw it. Let go of whether it's pretty or looks good. If you want to draw a table, don't go out looking for a table to draw, just draw it.

3. Keep going. Let go of whether it makes any sense. Just follow the energy and have fun.

4. Only use your eraser as a drawing tool. Don't obliterate, erase, or destroy anything just because you don't like it.

5. Keep going until there's nothing else you want to put in. We'll talk more about completion in the next chapter, but for now, just keep going until you've tried everything you wanted to try.

Get to Work and Get Inspired

Materials to Start:
- Your own self
- An attitude adjustment
- Time

Go back to the section of this chapter titled You Can Have Lots of Ideas. Reread the ideas listed there for exercising your divergent thinking muscles. Choose one. Do it.

TAKING IT FURTHER

Additional Materials
- Journal or notebook
- Pen or pencil

Now, take a little time to write about what you experienced. If you already have a notebook full of ideas, take some time to do the Conversation with an Overload of Ideas.

Chapter 8
Getting Engaged: Action

Commitment, Completion, and Challenge

Action is where the rubber meets the road, and you see where the road takes you. It is intentional, intuitive, and intense. It is a commitment to the process, to yourself, and to a goal that may take you places you never expected along a path you can barely see. This is where we take our artwork by the hand and give ourselves over to the dance of will and surrender.

You are asked to enter into artmaking as playful prayer with the mind of a novice, and as you go along in the process, you are invited to enter into ever-increasing levels of commitment. This is the moment where I start to murmur things about "for richer and for poorer, through sickness and in health," and your knees start knocking. This is where I ask you to stick with it even when the going gets tough. This is where I ask you to commit to completing your projects.

Artmaking, like life, is nothing if not a series of challenges. Getting engaged means making a commitment to stick with your artmaking through those challenges. If all of your artful explorations and projects are completely without challenge, then you aren't kept interested and you can't be truly engaged or fully in flow. Challenge is critical, as Csikszentmihalyi's research showed, for a state of flow.

Creativity is a process, it is a skill, and it is applied to solve problems. If there aren't any problems, then you're not really getting a chance to be creative; you're not applying your skill. Problems are part of what keep our lives interesting: What could I do to improve this relationship? How might I convince my boss that I deserve that promotion? How can I make room in the budget for skydiving lessons? What makes problems like these interesting rather than overwhelming is that we know we have the skills to solve them. What has the potential to keep us engaged in artmaking is that we are constantly running up against problems that are on the edge of our ability to solve; this is inherent in the very nature of artmaking as a spiritual practice. And yet it can be all too easy to quit as soon as we come to a challenge that feels a little out of reach.

It will not be possible to solve every problem you run across in an artmaking-as-playful-prayer adventure; what is possible—and important—is to resolve them. To solve means to find a correct solution; to resolve means to make a decision. You will not find that one right answer; you can, however, make a choice about how to move forward. You can commit to and reach a place of completion. Unresolved and incomplete projects just turn into mental and physical clutter.

Completion is not making it look good; it is not making it perfect; it is not even about getting exactly where you thought you would. Completion is not "being finished," as in refining or polishing. In fact, there is no external definition of completion. No one else can tell you if something is complete or not. Completion in artmaking as playful prayer is an internal emotional process as much as it is an external physical one. Completion is committing to and making the decisions you need to make in order to reach a fulfilling conclusion in the work.

Definition

Engage *Verb:* To assume an obligation, pledge, promise, contract, or oath; to become involved; to attract and hold fast; to fully occupy our attention and efforts.

Unless you try to do something beyond what you have already mastered, you will never grow.

–Ralph Waldo Emerson

Feeling Complete

So if completion is internal, and the result is a fulfilling conclusion, what does completion feel like? The more artwork we do, the more we come to trust our own instincts and recognize when resistance or perfectionism is at play. We begin to know when we're done with a piece, or when it needs to be set aside until later. All of us will experience completion in a slightly different way.

Sometimes, the sense of emotional completion doesn't happen until months after we're done working on a piece. It may take sharing the piece with someone else or displaying it before it feels complete. We may feel complete with a piece one day, only to dive back into it three weeks later with a fresh perspective. What follows are some common things people experience at completion. See if any of these resonate with you.

Generally, if a piece is complete, we'll feel a quiet sense of contentment, satisfaction, accomplishment, or even mild detachment. We may find ourselves inspired to try something different next time or it may leave us wanting to do more of the same. However, we rarely look at a piece that we are emotionally complete with and feel extreme emotions. If you do, you may be done working on it but find that you need to keep the piece out where you can see it, journal about what it means to you, or share the piece with a trusted friend and talk about the process you went through while making it.

When we consider a completed piece, nothing about it will feel missing or left untried. This doesn't mean it will be perfect; rather, it will be resolved. Generally, while a completed piece may leave us feeling happy or satisfied, a completed piece won't strike us as especially amazing or especially horrible. In fact, at a point of completion, we may feel that we can look at it objectively. I will often feel like something is complete when I can look at it and know I did the best I could with the skills and materials available to me in this moment. In completion, we can see the piece as a whole and appreciate it for what it is.

A completed piece has very little weight or momentum for the creator: It's not actively holding us back or pushing us forward. By their nature, incomplete pieces can feel like dead weight, sucking our energy and keeping us from doing anything else. Incomplete pieces can fill us with dread, guilt, or shame, emotions that can start an internal tug-of-war, pushing us away and pulling us in. Incomplete pieces can be seductively exciting, demanding our time and attention. Completed pieces lose this power, even if they remain "unfinished." If you've ever come across a long-forgotten, half-done craft project, you know what I mean. There may be a brief pang of guilt or sadness, and then you tuck it in the bag to donate and move on. You completed it when you made the decision to set it aside and forget it.

Completed projects have taught us all they can. Often, this is accompanied by a feeling of satisfaction or accomplishment: We've grown or learned something as a result of completing this project. The fact that the challenge is gone is part of why it can be easy to let go of completed projects. In fact, that ability to let go is another sign of completion.

Definition

Complete *Adj:* Having all necessary parts; whole; thorough.
Verb: To bring to conclusion or fulfillment; to reach an endpoint.

Accept that you have a million choices to make as a creative person, one after another... You must choose, and you must commit to your choice for exactly as long as it makes sense to commit to it.

–Eric Maisel

It can be tough to discern whether what we're feeling is completion or resistance taking the form of boredom or avoidance. I'll talk more about resistance and completion in the next chapter. For now, just remember that completion is usually accompanied by feelings of satisfaction, accomplishment, or contentment while resistance generally has a defensive or dissatisfied feeling.

Making Choices

So if we have to make decisions and take action in order to reach completion, how do we go about making decisions in artmaking as playful prayer?

We make decisions based on criteria. We may not be consciously aware of the criteria—in fact, we're often not. The criteria may be outside of our conscious awareness or may be based on emotional needs like "I'll do what makes me feel happy" or "I'll do what makes me feel safe."

If we have to make a more complicated decision, we may take the time to establish a set of criteria. These will be based on both our limitations and our ideal outcome. For example, if you want to get a bachelor's degree and are trying to decide where to go to college, you might come up with a set of criteria to evaluate the options based on what you want to study, how far away from home you want to travel, how much money you can spend, your current work and family commitments, etc. Your ideal outcome is a bachelor's degree in a particular field of study; your limitations include money, distance, work, family, etc. With product-oriented artmaking, we will have limitations based on our skill and our materials, and an ideal outcome based on the story we're trying to tell, the level of realism we're trying to achieve, or even the desires of the gallery curator or art teacher working with us.

With process oriented artmaking, we are letting go of an ideal outcome. While we still have the limitations of our skill, time, materials, and other resources, our only required outcome is completion.

With artmaking as playful prayer, the majority of our decision-making criteria are based on our intentions and our intuition. Hence the importance of setting our intentions right up front; they will guide every decision we make. Informed by our intentions, our intuition gives us a lot of strong hints about what to do. The risk is that then our intentions replace the ideal outcome. So that this doesn't happen, remember that an intention sets an attitude or course of action, not an outcome. We are making choices that will lead to the most appropriate action in the moment, not for some imagined and unknown future.

This also means that we are focused on discerning rather than judgmental decision-making. Discerning is about spotting differences; judging is about labeling things good or bad, right or wrong. There's a difference between using a small brush and using a large one: In artmaking as playful prayer, neither one can be considered right or wrong. There's just the one that might best serve our intentions and intuitive impulse in the moment.

He moves my hand. Do you think I would ever know how to do a picture like this by myself?

–Sister Gertrude Morgan, artist

Do not fear mistakes, there are none.

–Miles Davis

Anyone who has never made a mistake has never tried anything new.

–Albert Einstein

Great dancers are not great because of their technique, they are great because of their passion.

–Martha Graham

Here are a few simple questions to help you determine if your artmaking decisions are on track with your intention and intuition. Try asking yourself these questions aloud or in your head as you're working, especially when you feel stuck about what to do next or are having a hard time making a decision. If you're really stuck, pull out your journal and do some conversational journaling.

- **Am I in the moment?** If you need to ask, you're probably not. Try breathing, stretching, meditating or some other clearing activity and then coming back to the challenge—what solutions pop up?
- **Am I following the energy?** Generally, if you're bored or are doing something only because you think you should, it's not the best choice in the moment. However, the emotional energy behind the impulse doesn't have to be "happy"—sadness and even anger also carry a lot of emotional energy and can help guide your decisions. Even if an idea makes you angry, it may be worth exploring because of the energy behind it.
- **Does this serve the intention I set?** Consider your intention, and ask yourself if you're in that state of mind. Am I having fun? Am I staying present? If not, what decision might I make that would serve that intention in the artmaking?
- **Am I listening with my inner ears?** Often, when artmaking, we shout over our intuition. We may get an idea and shoot it down just because it doesn't fit with our logical idea of what we are supposed to be doing. Take a moment and give those ideas a chance.

As an artist, I can tell you that I have found it impossible to entirely dismiss the desire to make things that are pleasing to my eyes. The key is that I have also learned to follow the energy in my decision-making even if I have worries that the result might not be aesthetically pleasing. See what happens if you let go of making a beautiful painting as a criterion for your work.

Letting Go of the Story

Of course, letting go of the ideal outcome is easier said than done. In fact, it is extremely difficult to do. The bigger and more involved the project, the more likely it is that you'll get completely caught up in the story you think you're telling through the piece and start making decisions based on how well they fit the story. Or rationalizing your intuitive impulses and forcing them to fit the story. "Oh, cool, a domino! Nope, nope, can't put dominos in there, this is a jungle scene. Of course, jungles have leopards and leopards have spots, just like dominos…maybe I could have a few down here, like this…with legs."

And that's ok. It's a practice. We're following the energy, and we're tuning up our inner ears. The pure call of intuition may not come through every time we pause to make a choice about what comes next. If it doesn't, we just invite it along the next time.

A Conversation with Letting Go of the Story

If you're having a hard time getting the story out of the way, try one of these internal conversation or journaling techniques. Remember to listen for the inner voice.

Separate yourself from the piece. If the painting is its own entity, its desires are separate from yours. Forget what you want for a moment, and ask the piece what it wants. You can even try journaling this as a conversation. Try directing a few of these questions at the art itself, and see what you write down in response.

- What do you want me to do next?
- What do you need?
- Where are you incomplete?
- What do you want me to try?
- What color are you craving?
- Go with your first thought or impulse, even if it feels silly. Listen for the intuitive inner voice. The only guideline: Respect the work that you've already done and don't destroy the piece. You can paint over areas, rework things, or remove components. Deconstruct and reconstruct rather than trashing it.
- Ask yourself what you would do if the piece didn't have to look good. Would you do the fun thing, the scary thing, the crazy thing? What impulse would you follow?

A Note about Curiosity and What We Risk

"Hold on a minute," you're saying, "Following my first impulse is going to make the piece ugly. It'll be a crazy hodge-podge. I'm going to ruin it if I just follow every little impulse!"

And I'm going to ask you, "What's more important right now, following the impulse or having a beautiful piece?"

If having a beautiful piece is more important, that's fine! Go do that, and come back to this later. I simply invite you to make that choice because it's the choice you most want to make in the moment, not because you are afraid of making ugly art.

Doing this kind of artwork, we risk making ugly things. We risk seeing meanings we didn't intend. We risk telling a story we didn't control.

I recently had the opportunity to try avocado gelato—and didn't. What was the risk? I'm not allergic to gelato or avocados, the store was sanitary, I could afford it, and trying it wouldn't have alienated the people I was with. Still, I bought a scoop of pineapple mint instead. I didn't get the avocado, even though it sounded interesting. I could've had a scoop of avocado and a scoop of pineapple mint. I didn't. Why? Because in spite of the fact that I was curious about the avocado gelato, I was afraid I wouldn't like it. There was no real risk beyond an unhappy taste bud. Eating the gelato was not going to hurt anyone or endanger me. Now, I very much enjoyed the pineapple mint (as I suspected I might), and yet, months later, I am still curious about the avocado gelato.

Artmaking is one of those places where we can take risks in relative safety. We can experiment, learn, grow, play, and the risks we take are all manageable. With art, you don't even have to worry about the calories.

So what's the biggest risk we take with this kind of artmaking? We take the risk of making things we don't like.

And here's the big secret: It doesn't matter if you like it or not. It's not one of the criteria. There are colors I don't like to wear (yellow), foods I don't like to eat (Brussels sprouts), yet that doesn't make them good or bad; it certainly doesn't make them any more or less valuable. And I happen to think that yellow is a great color for walls, and that Brussels sprouts are really fun to draw.

Take a chance. Make some impulsive, intuitive decisions. Go with them and see where they lead, even if you think you might not like the outcome. There may be another, more valuable gift, lurking in the process.

Artful Explorations: Let Go of the Outcome

These next two Artful Explorations are both more complicated projects that can take a significant amount of time and use materials from the Intermediate Materials section, including acrylic paints. Acrylic paints are recommended because of the way they can be used to build up layers.

The What's Next? Art Jar

Materials

- Largish container you can put your hand into (like a box, bowl, or jar)
- Copy or notebook paper (to write prompts on)
- Scissors
- Pen or pencil
- Blank paper or sketchbook (larger and heavier weight is better)
- Junk mail, old magazines, old book pages
- Your favorite drawing and coloring materials
- Mod Podge or gel medium
- Acrylic paints
- Brushes and water container
- Rags or paper towels
- Permanent markers

OPTIONAL

- Wax paper or palette
- Gesso
- Colored construction paper

1. Choose at least 24 of the following phrases or art prompts. Write each phrase on its own slip of paper so that you can pull them one at a time out of the jar. You can handwrite each prompt or type the prompts into a word processing program and print them out. Either way, cut them up so that you have only one prompt per slip of paper.

2. Fold up each slip of paper and drop all 24 into your container. Mix them up. Get your art supplies ready and pull out a sheet of sketch paper.

3. Now, draw a slip of paper from the container and do what it says. Then fold the slip back up, put it back in the container, mix things up again, and draw another slip of paper. Again, follow the instructions. Repeat this at least 12 times. After the 12th prompt, do whatever you need to do to feel complete with the piece.

- Fill an area with a solid color
- Add a dotted line
- Add star shapes
- Collage three items onto the surface
- Add text
- Add a circle
- Put eyes on something
- Fill an area with a pattern
- Add red, orange or yellow
- Add blue, green or purple
- Add shading
- Add at least one collage element
- Add at least three straight lines
- Draw or scribble a shape, person or object
- Outline something
- Highlight something
- Add a rectangle
- Add a flowing line
- Add a reference to nature
- Add a reference to people
- Add blue or orange
- Add dots
- Add green or purple
- Use collage to add a pattern
- Do something to unify the space
- Rotate the piece 90° or 180° and choose a new prompt
- Find an element in the piece and repeat it
- Add egg shapes
- Add color
- Add one collage element
- Use a wash of gesso over at least ⅓ of the surface
- Use a wash of color over at least ⅓ of the surface

4. During each of the 12 rounds, you can do more than what's on the slip and you can do things that aren't on the slip. However, you have to do at least what's instructed on the slip of paper. There's a lot of room for creative interpretation of the prompts: stars could be movie stars and a pattern could be a dress pattern. Usually, I allow students to reject and redraw one prompt during the 12 rounds. The idea is to just keep working!

TAKING IT FURTHER

1. You may want to write up some of your own instructions and add them to the mix—"scribble," "crumple the paper and sand it," and "add bumblebees" are three of my personal favorites.

2. You can also keep the container, label it What's Next? and keep it nearby when you're working. If you have a stuck moment, you can always pull a slip and try doing what it says, just to keep the momentum going. Even noticing that you don't want to do what's on the slip of paper can push you in a new direction.

Artful Explorations: Let Go of the Outcome

Internal Journey Map

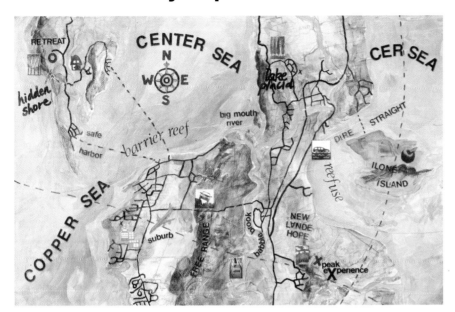

Materials

- Junk mail or old magazines
- Blank paper or sketchbook (larger and heavier is better; bristol board, watercolor board or scrap cardboard is ideal)
- Old maps
- Permanent marker (at least one, like a Sharpie)
- Mod Podge or gel medium
- Acrylic paints
- Brushes and water container
- Scissors

OPTIONAL

- Rub-on or press-on letters
- Gesso
- Rags or paper towels
- Wax paper or palette

1. First, pull out your sketchbook paper and your old maps. You're going to make a map of someplace you've never been. It might be completely imaginary, or it might be representative of something else in your life. The idea is to let yourself discover the place as you map it.

Piece together a base collage using your maps. Try using a crazy quilt collage of maps from different places and at different scales. You might leave blank areas for oceans, lakes, or parks. You might arrange them as a single city, a close-up of a region, or a map of the world with continents. Use Mod Podge or gel medium as an adhesive, and apply a top coat so that the acrylic paints will go on smoothly over the collaged maps.

2. (Optional) Once the base of collage maps is down, go over it with a wash of watered-down gesso. Apply the gesso with a very wet brush, or mix gesso and water about half and half and brush it over the surface. Then, wipe it back a bit with paper towels or rags. This way, while you can still see the maps underneath, there's a translucent white film over the top. It makes it easier to draw and paint on top of the maps, and blends the maps together a bit.

3. Begin painting and blending the map sections, emphasizing roads, rivers, water features, shorelines, cities, or other features and intersections.

4. When the paint is dry, you might draw roads in with a permanent marker. Does your map include symbols or need a legend? Do you need to label areas with names using rub-on letters?

Allow the idea that you will begin to make up a story about this place—and be willing to let go of the story and let the story change as you discover new areas and incorporate them into the map. You can take several days to do this, coming back to the map again and again, seeing new things and adding new things each time.

Super Simple Materials

- Blank paper or sketchbook
- Ballpoint pen or permanent marker
- Your favorite painting or coloring materials

Begin with your watercolors and paint some simple shapes. Let them become continents or city blocks, roads or rivers. Use markers, colored pencils, or a pen to add details and label areas, refining and defining the area you're mapping. Again, let yourself discover new things about this place as you work.

Additional Materials

- Journal or notepad
- Pen or pencil

Gather your pen or pencil and your journal or notepad and think about your life. Yup, this is a big one. Do some journaling and identify at least 10 big decisions, turning points, relationships, or phases in your life. Do any of those turning points or phases seem to be reflected in your map? Is there an additional legend or labeling system that you can use to add some of that information to the map? How is this different from or similar to the story you were making up about the place you were creating?

Chapter 9
Resistance, Judgment, and Completion

If you're going through hell, keep going.

– Winston Churchill

Resistance and Judgment

You've got a place to work. You've got your art supplies and your blank surface. You've read all about how to set your intention and get inspired and take action. You've reviewed everything you need to remember to stay in the artmaking process. And you're thinking that maybe now would be a great time to reorganize your kitchen cabinets so that the canned goods are in alphabetical order.

Okay, maybe that doesn't happen to you. I can tell you it sure happens to me. It happens to me not just around artmaking; it happens every time that I start out alone on a new venture. Practicing yoga. Going camping. Writing this book. Usually, I've taken a class, or read something inspiring, or done something fun with a friend, and decided I want to do more of it. I get all the supplies and then get completely paralyzed. Hello, resistance! Then I feel terrible, like a bad person, for not doing something immediately with all those expensive supplies. I beat myself up for it. Hello, judgment!

Judgment and resistance are like twin super villains, jumping in to gum up the works of the whole creative process. If you find yourself in a classic moment of resistance—too exhausted to make art, bored with what you're making, or determined to clean out the dust bunnies under the couch prior to sitting down to work on that collage— is judgment sneaking around somewhere, whispering in your ear? Is it pushing your inner frustrations out on others, telling you how your obsessive-compulsive boss makes you work too many hours, or that your housemate is a big dust-bunny-generating slob who leaves the house such a mess that you can't make any art? Or is it talking to you directly, using the voice of your inner critic to tell you, foolishly, that you don't know how to draw?

Curiosity: Antidote to Judgment and Resistance

Pat B. Allen has this to say about judgment in her book *Art Is a Spiritual Path*, "Judgments are inevitable and contain important information…information for ourselves…My judgment is a mirror of my values, my fixed ideas. When the image…calls forth my judgment, I have a chance to be curious." Judgment, like resistance, is a signal to us that something interesting is going on inside of us, just around the corner. Curiosity is an antidote to resistance and judgment. If we can cultivate an attitude of curiosity, then we are letting our own natural inquisitiveness guide us. Like the explorer and the adventurer, we can let go of an attachment or judgment and approach the world with playful wonder, open to whatever it has to share with us. With curiosity as our guide, we can let go of our ideas of how things ought to be and simply discover what's there. Like the novice, we can become eager to learn. Resistance melts away because we let go of predicting or judging what will happen and instead become excited to see what will happen next.

So, what would happen if instead of being angry or afraid of our critic, we approached the inner voice of judgment with curiosity? Much like a small child, the inner critic wants our attention and it wants to be in charge. Just as with that small child, we can be curious about what the child is saying while setting some very clear boundaries.

A Conversation with Your Critic

Try spending a little time in dialog with your critic, just as you have with your intentions and your artwork. I've found that journaling, physically writing down the conversation between my critic and my other self, is more useful than simply letting them chatter on in my head—or trying to force them to sit quietly in a closet. And it's a way of setting some boundaries. It lets me jump in with questions and guide the conversation based on curiosity rather than defensiveness, fear, or anger. Here are some great questions to direct toward your critic or inner judge when it starts spewing nastiness:

- What is the most important thing you want to share with me right now?
- What do you hope to gain by sharing that with me?
- What, if anything, are you hoping that I will do differently? (Usually, the judge has been triggered by something we're doing or thinking of doing, and it wants to stop us cold in our tracks.)
- What if I keep doing what I've been doing instead? How will that make you feel?

As you start asking these kinds of questions, you may discover that your inner judge is a control freak, or angry, or jealous. Nine times out of ten, my judge is simply scared.

Often, the concerns of the judge or critic are coming straight from a protective instinct, and they are working hard to keep us safe. Your job is to reassure the inner judge that while you refuse to indulge the hysterics, his or her most basic needs will be met. "We will still be loved and be safe even if I make an ugly picture." Once you've found out what unmet need or overwhelming emotion is behind the judge's outburst, you can go into another series of questions:

- If I keep doing what I've been doing, what's the worst that can happen?
- What might we do to make things okay again if that did happen? (or) What might we do to stay safe and get our needs met even if the worst happens?
- Great! Now that we know we can handle anything that goes wrong, will you please leave me alone for an hour (a day, a week, forever)?

So far, we've done this kind of conversational journaling with our ideas, with our selves, and even with our art, but it may feel silly the first time you try it with an imaginary segment of yourself. And you may just find it to be invaluable. With this method, we're not looking to kill off any parts of ourselves; we're looking to integrate them. We're assuming that every part of us is there for a reason and has something valuable to offer. The judge may just need some impulse control and a few lessons in mature behavior.

Through Resistance to Meaningful-ness

All art contains some element of self-expression. We are the ones making and we are the ones that the meaning is being expressed through; our personal mark will be on anything we make. Artmaking as playful prayer includes expressing ourselves and exploring our own lexicon of personal meaning. Yet to experience artmaking as a spiritual activity and as prayer, we need to allow meaning to emerge and be expressed in spite of ourselves.

Artmaking is a meaningful experience. Meaning happens in the moment, is experienced, and is then let go. The meaning is in the action of making and the product is just a record of that experience. Much of the resistance we encounter comes from trying too hard to be in control of both the process and the product; most of the deep engagement we experience comes from letting go.

When we engage in the process of making, meanings emerge that we did not intend. You may start out trying to create a shrine to a loved one that celebrates the positive impact they had on your life, and be shocked that you want to put a skull or a rubber rat in it. And it may stop you in your tracks. Interestingly, if you are doing artmaking as playful prayer, this is not the time to go into deep analysis and questioning. Nor is it the time to stop. This is the time to simply do it. Follow the energy, follow the impulse, and put the rat in. As I mentioned earlier, let go of the story and see what the artwork has to say.

Once, while painting an image of the Divine Feminine, I was disturbed by my sudden overwhelming urge to fill the image with phallic symbols. I managed to ignore the disturbance, painted the penises, and ended up with a painting I couldn't possibly have imagined. Similarly, I have watched students struggle with a shrine because they couldn't find a particular image or symbol, only to discover that something better appeared once they let go of their preconceived notions.

Meaning and symbols are complex and subtle. As much as some schools of art therapy and dream interpretation would argue with me, and as much as it is true that many symbols hold universal meaning, forcing meaning onto anything you make can kill what's trying to emerge. It is so tempting for me to say when I'm working on a piece, "Oh, those roots must mean X, so I should put in a Y because that would mean this other thing, which would be really cool." What happens, instead, if I listen—listen to the piece, listen to what was being said before all my analytical brilliance and ego and desire to produce something I can put up on my blog got in the way? Usually, it's something like "Mmmm. Roots. I like roots. I think I'll make more roots." Then, later, when I go back to the piece and gently inquire, I'll realize that the roots have turned into blood vessels and thread, and the potential meanings are more complex than anything my conscious mind might have come up with.

Definition

Meaning *Noun:* What is intended to be, or actually is, expressed; the purpose or significance of something; full of significance or expression in the moment.
Meaningful *Adj:* Having function, purpose, or significance in the moment.

An important time to paint is when you resist it the most. The strength of the aversion means that there is something just beneath the surface, thinly disguised, ready to emerge. Resistance is a reminder to probe your inner fears and defenses.

–Stewart Cubley & Michele Cassou

By practicing exploring meaning in our worlds, we are exercising our intuition and insight. We are gently unearthing our own language of symbols and images. We are expanding our ability to listen and communicate with Source. We know all of these things. And they're easy to forget. Making art helps us remember.

So When Is It Done, and When Is It Resistance?

As hard as it is to start a piece, it can also be hard to know when we're done. Often, we are lulled into thinking something is finished because we've filled the space, don't know what to do next, or have achieved some kind of equilibrium in the artmak-

ing. To quote *Life, Paint and Passion*, this is "when the real process begins ... when you run out of ideas, when you finally don't know what to do, when the path is narrow ... it is then that you have to dig deeper in yourself, to relinquish control ... [to] become the receiver rather than the doer."

As I discussed earlier, being complete brings on a quiet, satisfied, full feeling that I've done what I needed to do, explored every nook and cranny, and asked every question. Resistance—or the false ending—can feel like dissatisfaction, fear, dread, panic, anxiety, or boredom. It's when we say, "Oh this isn't turning out right, I'll just start another one" or "I'm so sick of working on this background." It's a tired, drained, static feeling. Resistance can also come in the form of pride and/or fear. If you're thinking to yourself, "I really love this banana I drew—it may be the best banana I'll ever draw" or "This looks like a real painting. I don't want to mess it up," it can keep you from moving forward. Resistance in that form can feel like a kind of mild panic or nervous excitement.

A Conversation with Resistance

If you're feeling panic, fear, or boredom, there may be something in the piece that wants to happen and hasn't happened yet. You may need to have a conversation with your piece like you did when letting go of the story or chatting with your critic. There may be something you wanted to do—and didn't—because it was too hard, too weird, or too risky. If you reach a stopping point and suspect this may be the case—or even if you don't—take a few minutes to ask yourself these questions:

- Is there anything you thought about putting in and didn't?
- Is there anything missing?
- Is there anything you were afraid to add?
- What might happen in the artmaking if you weren't afraid to ruin it?
- What's the biggest risk you could take with the art, while respecting what's already there?

If the answers to any of these questions fill you with a burst of energy, consider following the energy through the artwork to see where it leads. I have only one guideline: As I've mentioned before, whatever you do, respect what you've already done. If you cover over or deconstruct what you've already done, do it because something new has to happen, not because you want to destroy what's there. Violence doesn't break down resistance: It makes martyrs.

Over-Perfecting

For some of us, though, the challenge isn't stopping too soon. The challenge is not stopping soon enough. As many times as we tell ourselves that artmaking as playful prayer is not about the final product, we can get caught up in trying to make it perfect.

I have seen students reduce parts of their paintings to a mangled mush because they kept painting over and over an image, trying to get that one spot just right. In artmaking as playful prayer, you will be better off if you simply lay down the paintbrush and then let it go. You've made the mark; respect that it is what it is. Consider the notion that you can't change it or make it perfect, any more than you can erase a word once it's been spoken aloud. You can simply accept what is there on the page, and then make the next mark.

Making perfect art is not the goal of artmaking as playful prayer. Frankly, even the artwork made for product, the work we see in museums or galleries or eye jealously on the table in front of our classmates, isn't perfect. No piece of art will ever be perfect; it will simply be complete.

> ### A Conversation with Completion
> We talked in detail about completion in the last chapter. If you've considered some of the things that signal completion for you, add them to this list. If you think you're done, ask the piece, "Are you complete?" See what comes up. Then, do a quick check-in with yourself. Which of these ring true?
>
> - When you consider it, nothing feels like it is missing or undone.
> - You feel content or satisfied when you consider the piece.
> - Looking at the piece doesn't trigger any particularly intense emotions, like guilt, fear, or giddiness.
> - You have a sense of detachment about the piece. You may feel like you can see it objectively.
> - It no longer strikes you as especially amazing or horrible; it simply is what it is.
> - It is neither pushing you forward nor holding you back. It no longer has weight or momentum.
> - You have learned what you can from the project. You are ready to rest or to move on to a new challenge.
> - You can let it go.

All anybody needs to know about prizes is that Mozart never won one.

–Henry Mitchell

The only way through resistance is to embrace it— gently, respectfully, curiously. To live a creative life, we must lose our fear of being wrong.

–Joseph Chilton Pearce

Completion

Sometimes, the process of completion will happen naturally. Sometimes, you will need to make a conscious decision that something is complete, let it go or set it aside, and move on. This may happen if you've taken on an overwhelming project, are trapped in over-perfection, or are stuck with a project that is holding you back or that is laden with a lot of guilt or fear. Choosing to stop or set the project aside is one kind of resolution.

Be aware, however, that a stack of incomplete projects "set aside" can be a kind of mental clutter and a real energy drain; too many, and it's a sign of some serious resistance going on. Only you will know when it's time to be done with it and let it go or take on the challenge of seeing it through to a different kind of resolution.

Completion and Celebration

When you do reach completion in a piece, take a moment to pause. Too often in our lives, as soon as we finish one thing, we're off to work on another. We barely take a breath to check an item off of our to-do list before starting in on the next task. I want to encourage you to take the time to acknowledge what you've completed.

Celebrating the completion can be very simple. Make a note in your journal that you finished a piece. Describe it. Take a few sentences to note how it felt to work on the piece and how you knew it was done. Even say a quick "Thank you" to the piece for the gifts it gave you. Looking back in your journal after a year, you may be amazed by the amount of work you've completed! You can also take the time to do deeper journaling about each piece, exploring the challenges you faced with the piece and the messages the piece shared with you. If you live in a supportive environment, you may want to display the piece in a special spot, to be replaced by the next work you finish.

You can keep all the finished work in a big folder or on a special shelf, so that when you start to doubt yourself you can look back at the work you've done and see the progress. You may even find that a piece will look very different a month later than it did the day you completed it. You may also want to signal the completion of a piece with a bit of ritual or a special present. Light a scented candle as an offering of thanks or treat yourself to a sparkling apple juice toast. You may also decide to only make trips to the art store following the completion of a piece. This way, new art supplies become a reward for completed work, and not a substitute for artmaking itself.

Sometimes, though, it just doesn't feel like a celebration without other people. If you have friends who support your artmaking, definitely call them up to let them know you finished a piece so they can cheer you on! I'll talk more about building a creative community in the next chapter.

Lying Fallow

Making is a generative process, and we can't generate all the time. I've talked about goofing off and taking time to do the work of inspiration. There is another time we may need to take a break from active creating, and that's right after we've finished a big project. Nature goes through cycles and seasons, including times of intense growth and productivity and times of quiet when what remains breaks down into a base of nutrients that will support the next round of growth. Farmers who are in tune with natural processes and not reliant on chemical fertilizers let fields lie fallow; they also rotate crops to re-energize the soil. Sometimes, you too will need to lie fallow for a while and give your generative self a rest. It's okay to give yourself a little time to build up a layer of inspirationally rich topsoil.

Allies and Adversaries

Materials

- Deck of tarot cards (see note below for other options)
- Journal or notepad
- Pen or pencil

A Note on Using Tarot Cards: I do this exercise with tarot cards because the deck supplies a variety of archetypal symbols that most of us have strong associations with and that are rich with possible interpretation. Also, the simple chance involved in the selection process is a wonderful way of allowing ourselves to just be curious about the outcome. In these exercises, I have used images by Deva Padma from the Osho Zen Tarot

If you don't have a tarot deck or are uncomfortable using one, try using a book that includes images that have rich symbolism for you. For example, you might try randomly selecting pages from a book on ancient mythology, animals of the Southwest, yoga poses, or the unabridged plays of Shakespeare. How is the downward dog pose an ally or Medusa an adversary? The key is to select a book that is full of associations for you and to select the images or phrases randomly.

1. Take a few moments to consider the biggest challenge facing you in your artmaking. Write your challenge down in your journal in the form of a question, such as "How might I solve the problem of x?"

2. Now, shuffle the deck and select two cards, face down. Flip one of the cards over. For the purposes of this exploration, this card represents your Ally. (Resist the temptation to put the card back and try for something better!)

3. Now, be curious about your Ally. What are the qualities and features represented by the card? If you can, read up on what the card means. How might the strengths—or even the weaknesses—represented by this card support you in overcoming or solving your challenge? What could this card teach you? How could it help you? Take ten minutes and journal about the card and how it might serve as a valuable Ally.

4. Now flip the other card over. For the purposes of this exploration, this card represents your Adversary.

5. Be curious about your Adversary. What are the qualities and features represented by the card? If you can, read up on what the card means. How might the weaknesses—or the strengths—represented by this card be undermining you or making your challenge more difficult to solve? What could this card teach you? How does it serve as a mirror for you? Take ten minutes and journal about the card and how it might serve as a worthy Adversary.

6. Given what your Ally and your Adversary have shared with you, brainstorm 16 ways that you could answer the challenge. Remember, you phrased the challenge as a question for a reason!

Additional Materials

- 3 pieces of cardboard
- Copies of tarot cards you selected
- Mod Podge or gel medium
- Gesso
- Acrylic paints
- Brushes and water container
- Collage materials
- Scissors or craft knife

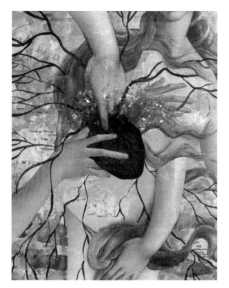

- Blank paper or sketchbook
- Your favorite painting or drawing materials

Consider making your own paintings or drawings of the Challenge, the Ally, and the Adversary. You can use your journaling and the tarot cards or other images as a starting point, and then see where the images themselves take you.

1. Consider making your own tarot cards to represent your Challenge, your Adversary, and your Ally. Start with three pieces of stiff paper or cardboard (old cereal boxes can be easily cut down to size). Try making them several times larger than an ordinary playing card so that you have plenty of room to work.

2. Now, sort through your collage images and pull things that make you think of the Challenge as well as images that might represent the Ally and the Adversary. You can even make copies of the actual cards you selected and use them as starting points for your Ally and Adversary cards. Either cut out the essential parts for use in your collage, or glue down the whole image and just gesso out the parts that you don't want to include. Then, add in other collage images that speak to you, allowing the cards to develop and change. You may find that your Adversary becomes your Ally, and vice versa. Let that happen. You're exploring.

3. Use acrylic paint to add in details or colors that emphasize the meaning for you. Again, be open to the meanings of the cards shifting as you work on them. One student worked hard on her Adversary card, working to convey a particular meaning, only to come to the realization that this actually represented a very real and beautiful strength of hers. She had worked with this Adversary since childhood and ultimately turned it into an Ally in her life without realizing it.

Critic Collage

Materials

- Journal or scrap paper
- Pen or pencil
- Junk mail or old magazines
- Other collage materials
- Blank paper or sketchbook
- Glue stick, Mod Podge or gel medium
- Scissors or craft knife

  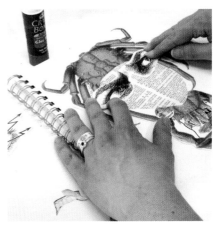

1. Grab your journal and your pen, and take a few moments to consider the voice of your internal Critic. What does the critic say? What tone of voice does it use? What kind of gestures is it making or body language is it using as it says those things? How does the critic make you feel?

2. Now, consider the possible physical characteristics of your critic—is it a particular color? Does it have a specific smell? What is the texture of its skin? Is it like a person you know, or an animal or insect?

3. Once you've spent some time journaling, get your collage materials. Pull out images that make you think of your critic or that have some of the same qualities as your critic. You may also pull images that inspire some of the same feelings your critic does.

4. Next, begin creating your critic. Consider what might comprise the arms or legs or body or head. The uglier and creepier the better!

Ultimately, the critic is a part of ourselves. Strangely, giving the critic its own body or face can make it easier to confront. Try talking to your critic. Does it seem a bit less powerful or a bit more ridiculous now? Are you more empathetic with your critic, or do you better understand its point of view?

SUPER SIMPLE OPTION

Super Simple Materials

- Blank paper or sketchbook
- Your favorite painting or drawing materials

Begin with the journaling as you would for the standard project. Then, start drawing or painting your critic. See what happens as the image emerges. Does it look like anyone you know? What additional or unexpected features are you inspired to include? Again, the uglier the better!

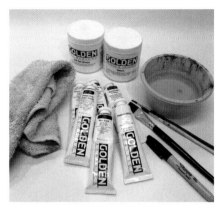

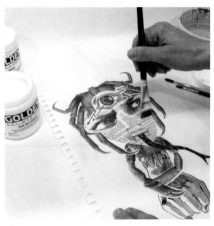

Additional Materials A

- Found objects, the more beat-up, the better—this might include things like old buttons, little screws, string, or bottle caps
- Thick craft glue like Tacky Glue or Ultimate Glue
- Permanent marker
- Brushes and water container
- Acrylic paint
- Gesso
- Wax paper or palette

A. You might choose to use some thick craft glue and add in other found objects or elements like bits of trash or string. You may also want to draw or paint on top of the collage to add details like beady eyes or claws or fangs or a monocle. As you can see here, I really had fun with the painting option!

Additional Materials B

- Old stuffed animals or toys
- Wire
- Drill
- Even more crazy found objects
- Heavy glue like E6000 or Goop
- Plaster bandages (like those used in mask-making, found at the craft store)
- Apoxie clay
- Acrylic caulk

B. This can also be a very fun project to take 3-D. Even if you've never worked sculpturally before, interesting things can happen. You can dismantle and reassemble second-hand stuffed toys or shape wire into fantastic forms. Small boxes can be glued or wired together and then painted and encrusted with found objects to create strange, ugly creatures. Any form can be covered with plaster bandages, texturized with acrylic caulk, or sculpted and shaped with Apoxie clay to add detail and cohesion to your creation. Making little critics is so much more fun than listening to them!

Here, I took the emotions that drive my critic—anxiety and fear—and made a little creature that utterly embodies those emotions. I used old stuffed animals covered in plaster bandage and acrylic paint to form the limbs, and used boxes covered with plaster bandage, Apoxie clay, collage and acrylic paint to create the body, face and container. The only limit is your imagination.

Chapter 10
Staying in Touch: Intuition

Listening for the Intuitive Voice

In the diagram of the flow factors that appears earlier in the book, Stay in Touch is in the very center. This is because it represents staying in touch with your deepest knowing and your own true self throughout the whole process. Artmaking as playful prayer really is about learning to listen for that inner voice, your own intuition, and giving it room to speak.

Staying in Touch is central because our intuition is involved in every piece of the process. Connecting with our intuition can happen at any point in the process (Getting Clear, Getting Inspired, Getting Engaged, or Giving Back) and can enrich every part of it. Becoming quiet enough to hear this inner voice, or the voice of Spirit, is part of what makes it both a conversation and a process of prayer.

You may notice that I don't distinguish between intuition and the voice of Spirit. This is because I believe that Spirit is always in us and is an essential part of us. Intuition is one of the ways Spirit speaks to us and through us; people also commonly experience Spirit through their bodies or their senses. If you find it uncomfortable to think of your intuition as a gentle nudge from the Universe, consider that it is a non-conscious assessment made from data and sensory input your body and brain have gathered and stored. Your intuition is the part of you that's paying attention to the big picture even when you're not.

Listening to that part of ourselves is what makes dialog with our art possible. So how do we learn to recognize the sound of our intuition, especially when notorious loudmouths like the Judge, the Critic, Logic, Fear, the Protector, or even Self-Preservation are cluttering up our mental airspace?

> **Definition**
>
> **Intuition** *Noun:* Gut feeling; a direct perception of truth; an immediate insight; instinctive knowing without conscious reasoning; the sound of the authentic inner voice or the inner voicing of Spirit.

I never paint dreams or nightmares. I paint my own reality. The only thing I know is that I paint because I need to, and I paint whatever passes through my head without any other consideration.

–Frida Kahlo

Tuning up Your Inner Ears

Tuning up our inner ears means learning to recognize the voice of intuition and Spirit. It sounds different and leaves us with a different set of emotions and sensations in our bodies than other mental chatter. I'm going to describe here some general qualities of the different voices as I, and others, report having experienced them during artmaking. As you practice tuning in, you may find that your different voices have their own unique qualities.

Our authentic inner voice leaves us with a feeling of opening, of possibility, of movement. It is the voice of our own creative power, our direct plug into the Universe. It is the giddy voice saying "What if?" It is the guiding voice that is in alignment with our highest purpose and the path of greatest learning—though it may not be easy or pretty. This is the place where the energy is flowing.

I found that I could say things with color and shapes that I couldn't say any other way, things I had no words for.

–Georgia O'Keeffe

The inner voice is, ultimately, a call to action, and so it can also have a restless tone. It lets us know when things aren't quite right with a nudge of discontent or discomfort. Usually this voice will speak out when we've gotten complacent or too settled in a routine. Yes, boredom can be a message from the Universe that it's time to do something different. And if we tune in, that feeling of possibility won't be far behind.

The intuitive impulse during artmaking isn't always positive—it can also have a tinge of anger or sadness. While doing a self-portrait, I may feel a strong impulse to put claws on my feet, a knife in my hand, and fangs curling out of my mouth. There can be a rush of excitement, and a sense of daring, to the impulse. "What if I showed myself as fierce? What if I were allowed to be angry?" Here's the key: The true intuitive impulse is usually followed by a sense of release, of opening, of freedom, of possibility. Artmaking is a safe place to explore and release feelings of anger or sadness, and our inner self will come to know this the more we make art.

The voice of our fear, on the other hand, leaves us feeling closed, stilted, trapped. Angry or sad impulses from this voice tend not to be followed by a sense of opening or release. Instead, they may leave us feeling guilty, shut-down, or ashamed. We can think of this as the voice of the critic, judgment, expectations, or old habits that no longer serve us. Frequently, this is the voice of the Protector, as theorized by Cynthia Wall in *The Courage to Trust*.

Wall describes the Protector as emerging to keep our most vulnerable child-self safe from hurt and discomfort. Usually, our adult selves can handle the things that would have hurt that tiny child, and the Protector is acting on habit and outdated information. We can handle a change in our routine, being left alone overnight, or criticized without feeling like the world will end. Impulses that come from the voice of fear or the Protector are constricting and tend to have a warning or threatening tone. "If you do that, you're going to get in trouble." "If you do that, you'll ruin it." We can learn valuable things from this voice, AND I advise against letting it guide our artmaking decisions.

Finally, there is the voice of instinct, of self-preservation. This voice goes deeper than the voice of our everyday fears—it is born of our own biological imperative to stay alive, to stay safe. It makes us flinch, back away, run. It can drive our need to eat or mate. Depending on the state of the world we grew up in and currently live in, we may have developed a sort of hyper-vigilance. We may not be able to distinguish our Protector from the voices warning us against real, life-threatening danger. Instinct and habit may have come together, making us extremely sensitive to small cues in such a way that we go into a mode of self-preservation at the slightest provocation. The fear that leads us to feel unsafe is different from the voice that speaks of guilt and shame, though for some of us, that line may be very thin.

Hopefully, none of the work you attempt as part of artmaking as playful prayer will make you feel truly unsafe. If it does, respect your own instincts. Take some time out to take care of yourself and then listen for the voice of your intuition, the voice

There is a vitality, a life force, a quickening that is translated through you into action and because there is only one of you in all time, this expression is unique. And if you block it, it will never exist through any other medium and will be lost. The world will not have it. It is not your business to determine how good it is nor how valuable it is nor how it compares with other expressions. It is your business to keep it yours clearly and directly, to keep the channel open…You have to keep open and aware directly to the urges that motivate you.

–Martha Graham, as spoken to Agnes DeMille

The painting has a life of its own. I try to let it come through.

–Jackson Pollock

THE CREATIVE CONVERSATION: ARTMAKING AS PLAYFUL PRAYER

encouraging you to grow and move. What does it say? Is there a way to be true to all of yourself?

The more you make art, the more you will begin to recognize the difference in these voices, and keep your inner ears open for the voice of Spirit.

Following the Energy

Intuition isn't always a voice or emotion. Our own energy level is frequently a signal from our intuition. It's just choosing to speak through our bodies rather than through our minds. Following the energy means following an impulse and keeping it interesting and fun for ourselves. This takes us in the direction of flow, of challenge.

Similarly, a dip in our energy may be a sign that what we're doing is no longer serving us. And that may mean shaking it up or changing the rules, just like kids will do in the middle of a game. Remember that this is supposed to be fun, at least most of the time. And fun is both relaxing and energizing. It doesn't have to be a woo-hoo, caffeine-rush kind of energizing—it can be a slow-battery-charging-I-want-to-do-more-of-this kind of energizing. Play is all about spontaneous, joyful learning … so have fun and follow the energy.

Your Intuitive Voice and Your Values

Another way to recognize our intuitive voice is that it will always be in alignment with our highest values.

So what are values? Values give shape to our needs, and our own personal ideas of what is the right thing to do. For example, as human beings, we all need food and shelter. However, based on our unique history, we may value a good job or strong family ties or education or thriftiness as ways of ensuring that our needs for food and shelter are met. We tend to give more worth to those things we value, and they develop a quality of inherent rightness.

Needs lead to values and values lead to actions. Since our actions stem from what we value, one of the quickest ways to check in on our values is to look at where we spend our money and where we spend our time. Pull out your checkbook and your credit card statements. Look over your day planner or your calendar. Every time I do this, I have to re-examine what I think I value and what my actions are telling me I value.

Our values are based in our needs as human beings; our intuitive voice speaks to our needs as spiritual beings. Our intuitive voice will always be in alignment with our values—it just may not seem like it at first.

I know I value spiritual connection, and I feel out of sorts if I don't do what I need for that to happen. If I've been feeling dissatisfied somehow, I may look back and realize that I've been spending all of my down time reading fantasy novels and watching police procedurals on TV. When I look more closely, I realize I need downtime and I value relaxation. After a long day, I realize that artmaking or going for a walk outside (two things I do to feel spiritually connected) feel like they take too much effort. A novel or a TV program meets that

The intuitive mind is a sacred gift and the rational mind is a faithful servant. We have created a society that honors the servant and has forgotten the gift.
–Albert Einstein

Definition

Value *Noun. A priority based on need and expressed through actions; the specific quality of a thing that determines its relative desirability, usefulness, or general worth; the inherent worth of a thing.*

Art, like morality, consists of drawing the line somewhere.

–G.K. Chesterton

need for relaxation much more easily. My intuition has let me know I need more connection time. Now I can set my creativity, reason, and common sense to work figuring out a way to both relax and get some of that spiritual connection I know I need.

And one of the things that our creativity, reason, and common sense help us do is set intentions. If our intention is in alignment with the values that are strongest in our lives, while serving the values we wish to develop and the intuitive nudges we're getting, it is more likely to feel "right." So when I set my intention to spend time in making art, I might say something like "I will relax when I make art today." We've got to meet our human needs as well as our spiritual ones.

A Conversation with Your Values

Take a few moments to consider the values listed on the next page. While no list can be all-inclusive, this list hits many of the highlights. Try rating each 1–5, where 1 means this isn't an important value for you at all, and where 5 means it's a very important value for you. There are no right or wrong answers. If you think of a value that's important to you that's not listed, write it in.

- Of those values you rated a 5, identify five to ten that you consider to be top priorities in your life.
- What needs are those top five to ten values supporting?
- How much time and money do you put into actions that support those values?
- Now identify the five to ten values that you spend the most time and money supporting.
- How are they different from the values that you consciously named as top priorities?
- What needs is that expenditure of time and money supporting?
- How might you adjust your actions so that both your spiritual needs and your physical and emotional needs are being met?

Values

Abundance	Inner peace	Openness
Giving	Self-care	Tolerance
Progress	Connecting	Efficiency
Acceptance	with people	Order
Gratitude	Integrity	Tradition
Prosperity	Self-reliance	Endurance
Accuracy	Connecting with Spirit	Passion
Grace	Intelligence	Travel
Punctuality	Service	Equality
Achievement	Consistency	Patriotism
Hard work	Intensity	Treading lightly
Quiet	Sharing	on the Earth
Adventure	Contentment	Excellence
Harmony	Interdependence	Peace
Relaxation	Silence	Treating my body well
Accountability	Cooperation	Excitement
Honesty	Joy	Perfection
Reliability	Simplicity	Trust
Being there for	Creating beauty	Exploring
loved ones	Justice	Personal growth
Honoring God	Skill	Unity
Resourcefulness	Creativity	Fairness
Calm	Knowledge	Personal honor
Honoring my family	and learning	Using all of my skills
Respect	Slowness	Faith
Challenge	Decisiveness	Physical strength
Honoring Nature	Leadership	and agility
Respect for authority	Solving problems	Variety
Change	Democracy	Finding beauty
Humor	Love	around me
Responsiveness	Spaciousness	Pleasure
Cleanliness	Discipline	Wisdom
Improvement	Loyalty	Flair
Restraint	Speed	Practicality
Collaboration	Discovery	Freedom
Inclusion	Making a contribution	Preservation
Romance	Spirituality	Fun
Comfort	Diversity	Privacy
Independence	Meaning	Any others?
Rule of law	Status	_____
Commitment	Doing new things	_____
Individuality	Modesty	_____
Safety	Taking action	_____
Communication	Economic stability	_____
Indulgence	Money	_____
Security	Taking risks	_____
Community	Economic success	_____

Artmaking as Conversation, Artmaking as Prayer

I've mentioned before this idea of artmaking as moving from self-expression to conversation to channeling. I've also mentioned that cultivating a conversation with your art is a key component of artmaking as playful prayer. Throughout this book, we've been engaging in all kinds of dialog with our art, our critic, and ourselves through conversational journaling. Being in dialog helps us follow the energy, keeps the momentum going, and makes it possible to move through the rough spots. After all, the voice of Spirit that we are listening for can speak to us through our minds, our hearts, our bodies, and the art we are making.

Now, I want to explore this idea in a little more depth. How do we listen? How do we have a conversation with a piece of art? Or perhaps more accurately, how do we treat artmaking as a dialog? The simplest answer is that we use our intuition to both listen and speak in this dialog. Yet most of us don't have enough experience really using our intuition to accomplish this easily. So, let's start by thinking of the artwork as a stranger we want to engage in a conversation.

In the brush doing what it's doing, it will stumble on what one couldn't do by oneself.

–Robert Motherwell

Consider for a moment how it is to meet a new person, someone you're curious about and find attractive or appealing in some way. You may notice them from a distance at first, delighted by the way their hands move in expressive and excited circles as they talk, or wondering at the small gold hoop looping through their upper ear. You may start with a few pleasantries, an introduction, the standard questions about what they do and where they're from.

Only when he no longer knows what he is doing does the painter do good things.

–Edgar Degas

You'll listen closely to the responses, your senses alert to subtleties and subtext. You are careful not to interrogate; your questions show a gentle curiosity and genuine interest in the other person. You may be surprised by some of the responses, some of what is revealed. You share things about yourself and begin to find connections, common ground. Perhaps you even allow yourself to be a bit vulnerable, sharing a passion or fear or experience that dips below the surface talk. You notice, you inquire, you listen. You find connections, you open up, you share.

This is exactly the same thing that happens when we are in dialog with a piece of art. We explore the materials as we start the piece. Maybe we start with a color of paint that's particularly compelling, a shape that feels good to make, or a collage image that excites our eyes. We pursue what's interesting. We use another color that makes the first vibrate, expand on the shape, or find other collage images that intuitively seem to fit with the first few. We keep working.

We notice what's beginning to happen in the piece—we don't analyze, we don't interrogate: We listen. We may say to the piece, "What are you trying to tell me?" or "What do you have to teach me?" or "What do you want to share?" We've already begun doing this when we hit a challenge; now we can consider making it a part of our ongoing process. We can do this talking in our heads, in a journal, or even on the back of the piece.

You may begin to notice that the colors remind you of a vacation you took two years ago in New Mexico, or the shapes make you think of a jungle, or the eyes of the shampoo model in your collage make you think of your sister and that time she did a belly splash in the neighbor's pool. You may begin to see the shape of little adobe buildings in the splashes of watercolor, or turn the jungle shapes into tiger eyes, or dig through your collage materials for more images of water, children, sun umbrellas.

The entire conversation is intuitive. We are noticing the things that happen in the artwork, open to whatever might happen, ready for the unexpected. Intuition is using our eyes, our ears, our hands. The energy and excitement stay with us because there is an element of exploration, of discovery. You may return to the peace you felt during that sun-drenched vacation, wonder at the unknown that is both terrifying and mysterious, or decide that it's been way too long since you talked to your sister. And then it may go in a completely different direction. You may find yourself painting pyramids or including images of roses just because they feel right. Observe what unfolds and let go of controlling it.

And this is how our worries, our troubles, our desire for a spiritual connection will have room to speak during this process. This process leaves space for Spirit to speak to us in subtle ways through our own inner voice and impulses. And this is how our artmaking has the potential to become the kind of conversation that is prayer.

A Conversation with Your Intuition

In many ways, this entire book is an exercise in building up the strength of our intuition and learning to recognize and trust that inner voice. It is about learning when to exert our will, push through and actively problem-solve: It is about learning when to surrender to Spirit, listen, and gently follow the impulses.

Through the course of this book, we've talked about a number of ideas that support and strengthen our ability to hear that inner voice. In the beginning of the book, I described them as the attitudes and actions that make up the work of art, that make art a verb. Most of these we've already covered in some depth; a few will appear in future chapters. Right now, grab your journal and take a few moments to consider your own inner voice and the actions and attitudes of artmaking.

> *Art is a collaboration between God and the artist, and the less the artist does the better.*
>
> *–André Gide*

12 ACTIONS AND ATTITUDES OF ARTMAKING
Explore
Focus on Process, Not Product
Defer Judgment
Be Like a Novice
Be in Conversation
Be Mindful
Follow the Energy
Let Go of the Outcome
Be Curious
Tune Up Your Inner Ears
Cultivate Appreciation and Gratitude
Hold Clear Intentions

- Of these 12 actions and attitudes, which ones are easiest for you? Which ones come naturally?
- Which ones do you find to be extremely challenging or difficult?
- How does your inner voice most frequently speak to you?
- How do you distinguish between the voices of intuition, fear, and self-preservation?

Value Collage

Materials

- Junk mail or old magazines
- Glue stick, Mod Podge or gel medium
- Scissors or craft knife

OPTIONAL

- Cutting mat
- Blank paper or sketchbook
- Acrylic paints
- Brushes and water container
- Wax paper or palette
- Gesso

1. This process begins much like the process for the Discard Collage from Chapter 1. Start by going through your stack of junk mail for the day, the contents of your recycle bin, or a stack of magazines you're ready to give away. If you've developed a collection of collage materials, go through that, too. Give yourself no more than 15 minutes to explore these materials, keeping your eyes open for things that are visually interesting to you or things that grab you in the moment—words, pictures, patterns, textures, colors—and rip them out. Don't analyze your decisions; just rip the images out and set them aside in a stack.

2. At the end of the 15 minutes, look at what ended up in your stack. Begin sorting the materials. What patterns emerge? Are there common objects, images, feelings, symbols, colors, textures? Group the images, making 3–5 separate groupings. Don't read any further yet, just sort your images.

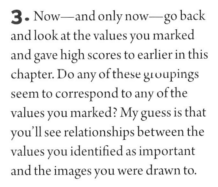

3. Now—and only now—go back and look at the values you marked and gave high scores to earlier in this chapter. Do any of these groupings seem to correspond to any of the values you marked? My guess is that you'll see relationships between the values you identified as important and the images you were drawn to.

4. Now, take scissors and a glue stick and begin to make a collage from each of the groupings. See if you can center each collage around a value or cluster of values. Feel free to add additional materials or rearrange groupings to more fully express the value. Let your conscious discernment and your intuition dance in the process of making.

5. You may find that one or two of the collages capture your imagination, or take you off in an unexpected direction. That's ok. Feel free to bring paints or other media into the mix to follow the image where it leads you. (A group of images that I recognized as relating to trust went off in a completely different direction with the image here.)

SUPER SIMPLE OPTION

Super Simple Materials
- Blank paper or sketchbook
- Your favorite painting or drawing materials

1. Begin by imagining your ideal day, ideal place, or your ideal self. Take a few moments to consider it. Is there a color, object, animal, symbol, or feeling that seems to dominate?

2. Start painting or drawing that color, object, animal, symbol, or feeling. The objective is not to recreate the ideal you imagined; it is to create a painting that uses some impulse from that ideal as a starting point. Use the techniques from Chapter 7's Just Draw Just Paint Exploration. Allow the painting to develop and emerge, following the impulses.

3. Once it feels complete, go back to your values list and see what got the highest scores. How does the painting reflect those values? Are there any surprises?

TAKING IT FURTHER

Additional Materials
- Journal or notepad
- Pen or pencil

After you've finished a collage or a painting, take a few moments to write about the piece, either on the back of the collage or in a journal. You might consider writing about the patterns that emerged, what surprised you, or the values that became the focus of the pieces.

Matchbox Assemblage

Materials

- 6–12 empty matchboxes (these can usually be found at the grocery store near the paper plates and other picnic items—I used mini matchboxes in this exercise, but feel free to use the larger ones if they appeal to you)
- Junk mail and old magazines
- Other collage materials
- Mod Podge or gel medium
- Heavy craft glue like Tacky Glue or Ultimate Glue
- Small found objects (things that will fit in a matchbox like keys, shells, etc.)

OPTIONAL
- Gesso
- Brushes
- Acrylic paints
- Wax paper or palette
- Cigar box or heavy cardboard (to mount or arrange matchboxes)
- Tiny brads or buttons (can be used as handles to open matchbox drawers)

1. To begin, gather some of your favorite small collage images and small found objects. Begin sorting and arranging them. Are there themes that emerge, such as common colors, shapes, textures, or symbols? Are there objects and images that you are drawn to and collect? Find at least three themes or groupings of images and objects. You may have more groupings, or you may choose to do more than one box for each theme.

2. Next, prep your matchboxes, at least one matchbox for each theme or grouping. You might choose to paint the exterior of the box with gesso. This way, the exterior of the box is a clean slate for whatever collage materials or paint color it needs. You can leave the interior and exterior of the little drawer unpainted so it's easy to open and close, though painting the interior of the drawer with gesso can also make it easier to paint with color if need be. (The color will be more vibrant on the white gesso than on the grey cardboard).

3. Now, using at least one matchbox for each theme, begin arranging the images and objects on and in the matchboxes. You might paint the exteriors of the boxes or use Mod Podge or gel medium to collage imagery on the outsides.

4. You can fill the drawers or create carefully glued arrangements using Tacky Glue or Ultimate Glue to secure the objects. You can attach tiny brads or buttons to the outer edge of the drawers so that you can more easily open them.

5. Each box might be its own tiny shrine, or you might choose to arrange them one atop the other like a chest of drawers, or arrange them in a larger box. You might also decide to arrange them on a piece of board so that the matchboxes become part of a larger, interactive collage that can be hung on the wall. Whatever you do, consider leaving the drawers so that the interiors can be opened and explored.

6. Consider each little matchbox as a message from your intuition—what secrets do these objects and images whisper to you? What meaning do they hold?

Additional Materials

• Old hardbound book with a ¾" spine (one that you feel okay about taking apart)

It is also possible to arrange the matchboxes inside an old hardback book. You can cut through the pages to make slots for the matchboxes, or remove all the pages and glue matchboxes inside where the pages used to be. Placed on a bookshelf, the matchboxes are completely hidden.

Chapter 11
Giving Back: Community

About Community

We have spent much of this book talking about *getting*: Getting Clear, Getting Inspired, Getting Engaged. You have been actively gathering creative energy and insights and now is the time for me to gently nudge you to share the wealth. Let me assure you that "sharing the wealth" does not mean you have to have an art show in a gallery, or start selling your work, or even show your friends what you've been working on, though you certainly can. It does mean looking up from your own work and realizing that your artmaking is not happening in a vacuum.

Community In-Person

It's not a coincidence that monks and nuns often live in groups, or that many spiritual traditions include regular meetings with others. Consider community mural projects, life drawing sessions, church choirs, quilting bees, and even knitting night at your local coffeehouse. Doing creative and spiritual things with a group of other people helps us stay committed, and it helps us build and develop our own practice. We learn from each other, are inspired by each other, and are challenged by each other.

> **Definition**
>
> **Community** *Noun:* A group of individuals who share a common purpose or similar interests, often within a geographic area; a group of people whose connection is maintained through sharing and the exchange of ideas and resources; a fellowship or society; something in common possession or enjoyment.

While this book is designed so that you can use it on your own, you can easily do the explorations with a friend, have art project days with a small group, or use an online forum to share and discuss the work. In fact, there are so many advantages to group work that I don't offer much in the way of one-on-one coaching anymore: I focus on offering workshops. It's also why I have spent a lot of time over the past few years developing my own communities of practice.

Fresh out of college, I sold batik on the craft show circuit. I would see the same people at events from Washington to California, and we would share resources, talk technique, and commiserate about the weather. Even though we were all very different and made different kinds of arts and crafts, we had a set of experiences in common and a pool of mutually beneficial knowledge to share. As determined a loner as I was, I really loved the sense of community I felt.

The work that I am doing now doesn't lend itself so naturally and easily to the development of community. So, I have worked consciously to connect with other artists, teachers, activists, and seekers; these others also see creativity as part of their spiritual path and community service.

You can probably think of a few people you know who would be game for a night of collage and conversation. There is probably a process-oriented art class you could take nearby or a workshop you could attend in the next few months. Check the resources section at the back of this book or on www.eyesaflame.com for instructors, methods, and workshops that take a process-friendly, spiritual, and/or personal growth approach to artmaking. If you work as a healer or an artist, there might be a professional organization you could join. If you are involved in a faith community, there may be a choir, art committee, or other creative group you could explore. Spending face-to-face time in creative spiritual community is invaluable.

Community Online

Of course, spending time alone is valuable, too. As a self-avowed introvert, I spend a lot of time alone. Though I no longer live alone, I do most of my work alone at home. I love going to dinner or a movie by myself. And yes, I spend a lot of time making art alone. Sometimes, the idea of going out to a party or attending a meeting gives me the heebie-jeebies.

And this is why I love the Internet. I'm not suggesting that it's a substitute for the face-to-face experience of creative community, and I understand that some of you may be cringing at the idea of anything Divine being expressed through Facebook. Yet this, and a huge variety of other Internet tools like Twitter, blogs, and photo-sharing sites (some of which are described in the resources section on www.eyesaflame.com), give introverts, the homebound, and people stuck working in cubicles for 12 hours a day the opportunity to engage in community.

Definition

Sharing *Verb*: To participate in, enjoy, or experience with others, jointly or in turns; to relate a story or experience to another; to divide and distribute portions.

I love that if I come across an inspiring quote, a beautiful image, or a challenging question during my workday, I can share it on Twitter or Facebook and then hear back from other like-minded teachers, artists, and seekers. I have another friend who accomplishes something similar through a more targeted email group. Several times a day, I'll get notes from her with information on great artmaking opportunities, spiritually oriented events, or a cat needing a new home. Each of us, in our own way, is giving back to and engaging in our community without ever leaving our desk chairs.

Whether in person or online, what you choose to share is up to you. It may be enough in the beginning to share your time with others in a setting that supports creativity by attending a workshop or following another artist's blog. You may choose to share your experiences, feelings, or ideas, or even resources or materials. You may come to a place where sharing your knowledge, expertise, or just a cool technique you've learned feels like the right thing to do. You may decide to participate in a creative swap, or host a knitting night, or organize a group that meets regularly.

You might also decide to channel your creative energy into volunteering, activism, or charity. I taught craft classes at a residence for women in transition from homelessness, and I have an aunt who knits shawls for cancer patients. Currently, I volunteer with a local arts organization that has a focus on community education. You may decide to volunteer in the arts program at your kid's school or get involved in a program like Afghans for Afghans.

Art and craft have a long history of being applied as tools for activism and social change, and using your creativity in service of a cause you believe in is another way of giving back. To get you started, I have included information on a few resources for getting involved in art and craft activism in the resources section of www.eyesaflame.com.

Appreciation and Gratitude

The simplest way I know of to share, and to build community, is to cultivate an attitude of appreciation and gratitude. Many of the Artful Explorations in this book are also exercises in appreciation—in being deeply present and noticing the beauty and value in what's around us. If you decide that part of your creative journey will be to draw or paint the things you see in the world around you, the first step is appreciating them.

People also respond very well to appreciation. It's amazing what can happen when you notice the things that make people special and thank them for what they do. I have a friend who, on her birthday, invited a small group of friends for brunch. We came out, happy and ready to celebrate her, and then were shocked into a sweet silence as she proceeded to read aloud a paragraph for each friend, full of the things she appreciated about each of us. I was amazed by what she saw in me and delighted by what I saw in her.

Remember, too, that appreciating is different from liking. I can be grateful that my friend loaned me a yellow sweater on a cold day, recognize that she made a good point during that discussion, or value the care and attention that went into the meal she made—and not like the sweater, the point, or the meal. Yet, in every case, I've been able to see the value of the exchange and so am ready to return the favor. I'm ready to share, and that builds community.

In fact, your own artmaking could probably use a little bit of this. Are you acknowledging the value of your own work and your own process, or are you demanding a particular outcome? Are you saying "Thank you" for what the piece has to offer and the beauty that is there, even if it's as simple as "I really appreciate that shade of red right there in the corner" or are you complaining about what isn't there? This kind of appreciation can also be another way of celebrating completion.

Definition

Appreciation *Noun:* Recognition of the quality, value, or significance of people or things; an expression of gratitude; an increase in value over time.

A Conversation with Appreciation

Take a few moments to consider a situation, event, finished piece of art, or even a person you find hard to appreciate or feel gratitude for. Remember that appreciation is a type of deep noticing, looking beyond the surface. Pull out your journal and ask yourself the following questions. Using conversational journaling, see if you can find something to appreciate. With appreciation, these things increase in value over time.

- What did I learn from this?
- How might others benefit from this?
- What did it have to share with me? What did it offer freely?
- What else has become possible because of this? What doors have opened?
- What might be considered beautiful about it?

Do I Really Need to Get Other People Involved in This?

Certainly, simply by the act of creating, we are already sharing with and communicating with Spirit. For the shy and retiring among us, it may seem unreasonable that we also need to go out and involve other people in the whole thing. The simple truth is that part of how Spirit communicates is through us to each other. We are part of how the Divine acts and communicates in the world. If creativity is going to be a part of

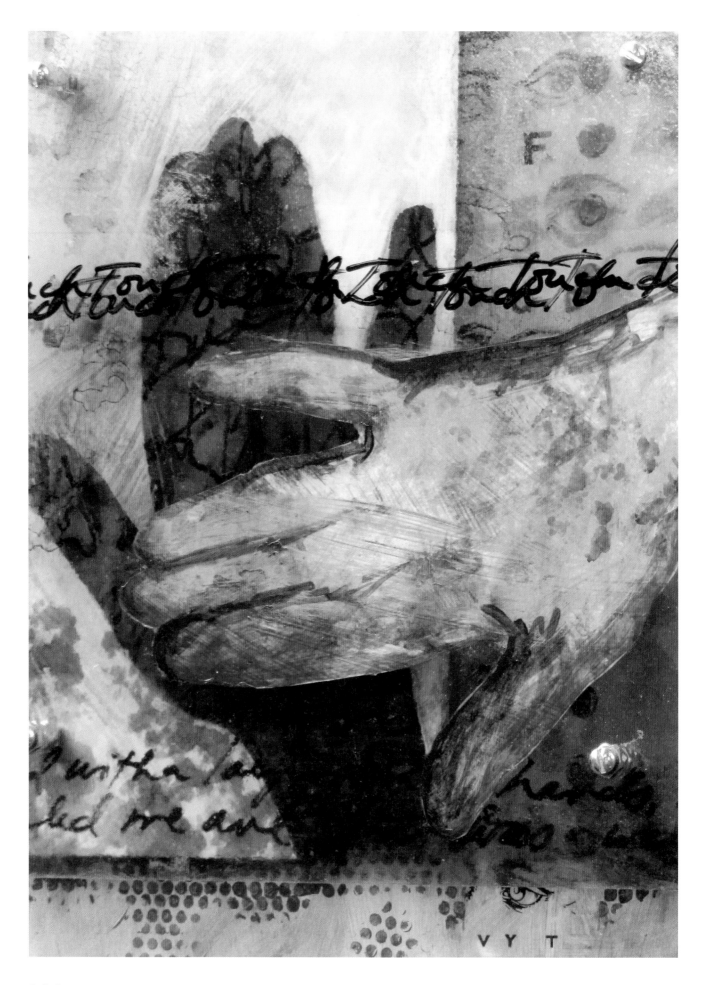

THE CREATIVE CONVERSATION: ARTMAKING AS PLAYFUL PRAYER

your spiritual path, then creative community of some kind will also be a part of that path. Naturally, it manifests differently for everyone.

Being in community is not easy for everyone. It is not always easy for me. I can be an impatient know-it-all, and I can get overly caught up in making people laugh and forget to listen. I can be distracted from the present by my desire for approval or my worry that people don't like me. I can get worn out from being over-stimulated. And yet, being in community is exactly how I've learned that all of those things are challenges for me. And it's where I get to practice doing things differently.

Likewise, it is in the context of creative and spiritual community that I have learned all of the things I'm able to share with you now. And it is in the context of community that I am sharing these ideas with you, so that you now have the opportunity to discuss them, adapt them, and figure out what, if any of it, suits you. And it is in the context of community that anything you do will be applied.

And this is what Giving Back is all about. If this is a spiritual practice, then part of the intent in practicing artmaking as playful prayer is to learn and grow. And part of the intent in learning and growing is to be a little more conscious in our daily lives. I believe that making art and teaching art in this way has helped me be more conscious, and I believe that I have been able to more often interact with others in a loving way. Not all the time, not every time. Just more of the time.

Thank-You Notes

Materials

- Blank cards and envelopes (you can get these at a craft store, or make your own blank cards from heavy sketch paper or construction paper—folded paper can be also be used as an envelope)
- Glue stick or Mod Podge
- Old Artful Explorations projects
- Scissors or craft knife

OPTIONAL

- Colored construction or origami paper
- Photocopies of your artwork

1. Pull together at least ten blank cards with envelopes. You can purchase cards at the craft store, or you can make some cards and envelopes from paper you already have. Do an online search for "making your own envelopes" to find free templates, or take apart an envelope of the right size to make your own template.

2. Now, look through the Artful Explorations you've completed. You probably have some collages, maybe a drawing or two, and some glue doodles or other paintings that you're not attached to and even considered throwing away. Yet, each of these pieces represents some hard work and attention on your part and it's time to share.

3. Use your cardboard camera from the exploration in Chapter 1 to scan the pieces and identify interesting compositions or components. Consider cutting up the original works to free these little gems or art fragments. You may also want to make photocopies of the original works, and cut up the copies instead. Pieces that are at least 2" square work well. Keep working until you have at least as many art fragments as greeting cards.

4. Now, glue these art fragments to the fronts of your greeting cards. You can glue down a piece of colored construction paper or origami paper first to create a frame or accent for the art fragment. You can also combine multiple fragments to make more complex arrangements.

TAKING IT FURTHER:

Additional Materials
- Pen or pencil
- First class stamps

A. Now, think of several people who could do with some appreciation and gratitude. Thank-you notes are not just limited to expressing gratitude for gifts after a holiday or birthday. You might send a card to someone who has gone out of their way to help you or someone who gives of themselves on a regular basis. Consider which card might appeal to each person. Over several days, take some time and write a thank-you note to each of them. Be specific: Say exactly what you appreciate about them. Hand address and mail them. Finally, write one to yourself.

B. Keep the cards on hand for when you feel the impulse to send a thank-you note. Thank-you notes can go out anytime, for anything. Some people extend this practice and make a point to send out a thank-you note every week or even every day. Not all of them need to be handmade, but sending a little bit of yourself along gives the gesture extra meaning (even if the person doesn't know you made the art!).

Paper Prayer Beads

In Tibetan Buddhism, prayers are written on wheels and printed on flags—a person spinning the wheels or the wind moving the flags is thought to activate the prayers and send them out to Divine ears. In the Catholic tradition, a beaded rosary is used to not only symbolize and promote meditation on the mysteries of the Christian faith but also to aid the worshipper in tracking prayers as they are said. Hindus use strings of prayer beads to count mantras as they are repeated, as do some Buddhists and Muslims. Consider your own beads, what they might symbolize, and the different ways you may want to allow the messages in the beads to be remembered or activated. They can be strung together as a curtain or necklace, stitched to an altar cloth, or incorporated into a shrine.

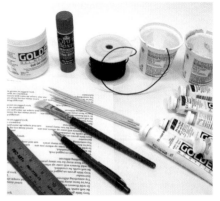

Materials

- A poem, prayer, gratitude or inspirational phrase
- Pen
- Ruler or straightedge
- Glue stick
- Mod Podge or gel medium
- Paint brush
- Scissors or craft knife
- Bamboo skewers
- Blank paper or sketchbook (blank or lined on at least one side, and at least 1" wide and 8" long)
- Two old cans or yogurt cups
- Old newspaper

OPTIONAL

- Blue painter's tape
- Colored construction or origami paper
- Cord, string, or necklace chain (no thicker than your skewer)
- Acrylic paint
- Water container
- Wax paper or palette (optional)

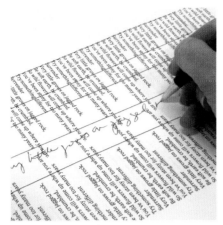 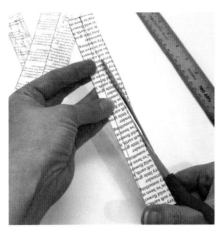 

1. You're going to be writing your poem, prayer, or inspirational phrase on long triangles of paper, and then rolling them up. I recommend using strips of paper that are at least 1" wide and 8" long. You can use your home printer and regular printer paper, printing your words out on the paper in a repeating pattern or you can mark out areas 1" × 8" and fill them with your own handwriting. You can write on one side of the paper or both. Either way, it will be easier if you get the words onto your paper before you cut the triangles out. With this project, it's not important that the words are legible once the bead is formed; it's simply important that the words are there.

2. Next, trim your 1" × 8" pieces of paper so that they are long triangles. It helps if the point is centered, but not necessary. These can be free-form triangles!

3. Take the widest end and roll it once or twice around your bamboo skewer and secure that first bit with a dab of gluestick. You can use just about any thin tube to roll your bead on—I've just found that the diameter of a bamboo skewer is good for beads, and the length makes it easier to work with. Your writing can be on the inside or the outside of the roll—naturally, it will show more if it is on the outside, but either way it will be more pattern than legible text.

4. Next, with the end of the paper securely rolled around the skewer, brush a thin coat of Mod Podge over the remaining triangle. Now, roll the paper up, glue side in. Wipe away the excess Mod Podge (I usually use my fingers, and try to use the excess glue to seal the surface) and slide the bead off the skewer. Doing this on old newspaper will keep your workspace less sticky!

5. To let the beads dry, just put them on another skewer raised up off the table's surface. Here, I've balanced mine on two notched yogurt containers.

6. You can also use this kind of a set-up to paint the beads with a thin wash of acrylic paint if you want to add color. To seal them, coat the surface with a thin layer of Mod Podge or gel medium. Here, I've secured the skewers with blue painter's tape to keep them from spinning and rolling.

7. Make as many beads as you like, using different phrases, words, poems, or inspirational phrases. Even if the words are illegible, the beads serve as a subtle reminder of the message they contain.

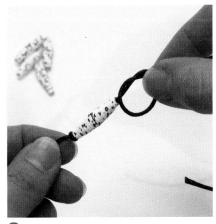

8. The beads can most simply be strung on a cord. Just make knots at the ends and in-between the beads to hold the beads in position.

Additional Materials

- Small stones
- Tiny rubber stamp letters
- Staz-On® stamping ink pad
- Other pretty beads and jewelry-making tools (optional)

A. You can also combine the handmade prayer beads with commercial beads or other found objects and tokens to create a more varied or meaningful composition. Here, I've included beads and charms from my own collection. Jewelry-making books may also give you additional ideas for construction and tools.

B. You can also make prayer beads out of other materials. It's possible to find pre-made beads that are large enough to be decorated with collaged images and text.

If you want to learn more about prayer beads, including their history and meaning, and how to make more elaborate sets, I recommend the book *A String and a Prayer* by Eleanor Wiley and Maggie Oman Shannon.

C. You may also find a worry stone to be useful. This small, smooth stone can rest in a pocket, within easy reach if you need a quick reminder. A smooth river stone can be painted or rubber stamped with a reminder word and tucked into a pocket on difficult days.

Chapter 12
Maintaining ArtMaking as a Spiritual Practice

Practice means to perform, over and over again in the face of all obstacles, some act of vision, of faith, of desire.

–*Martha Graham*

Now that you have read through the book, maybe tried some Artful Explorations, worked on your own or with a group, and put a foot in the waters of artmaking as a spiritual practice, you have come to a decision point. Is the practice of artmaking as playful prayer something that you want to continue to do regularly, something you want to build into a habit in your life? Or has artmaking just been an interesting learning experience that you feel ready to leave behind?

There is no right answer. And you may even find that the answer shifts and changes as time goes on and you integrate your various experiences. You may also decide that while visual artmaking is not a creative path you want to pursue, a regular creative practice like knitting, sewing, writing, dancing, gardening, or cooking can serve the same role in your life. There are many ways to put the principles into practice if they call to you.

The key is to decide what you're going to do, and then commit to doing it regularly.

If you've read the first chapter, you'll know that much of my life has been a struggle with discipline. Even working on this book, I have had to do a number of things to hold myself accountable and keep engaged through completion. I have had to schedule special writing times, take writing retreats, work with a writing group, and give myself firm deadlines (many of which I missed!). I still tend to work in fits and starts: I am not the person who wakes up at 6 am every day and writes for three hours. And still, you're holding this book in your hand, so I must have managed to get it done!

I have tended to think of discipline as a punishing thing, like getting a spanking when I forgot to turn off the light in my bedroom—or a boring thing, like reading three chapters in a chemistry text every night before bed—or a painful thing, like doing 20 push-ups every morning no matter what.

When I started thinking of discipline as doing something regularly so that I learn it, so that it becomes second nature, my perception shifted. I wasn't going to be punished if I didn't do it, whatever "it" was that I needed to be disciplined about. "It" was just going to get easier if I did it regularly, and I'd be more likely to experience the benefits the practice had to offer. Now, discipline for me is about being in integrity with my intentions—and doing the work. I still struggle with discipline, but it has become something much more positive in my life.

If you choose to consider taking on a creative discipline going forward, it may also help to think of those practices as rituals. Framing your morning cup of coffee and journaling as a ritual to honor your creative self may feel more in alignment with your own values as well as being easier and more fun to do than "I have to write every morning if I want to be creative."

Practice what you know, and it will help to make clear what you do not know.

–*Rembrandt*

Definition

Discipline *Noun:* A regular practice that leads to learning; training; an area of study or focus; regularly repeated action that forms habits; a ritual process leading to spiritual discovery and insight.

Intention and Action

If you want to consider incorporating a regular creative ritual into your life, first consider what your intention is.

Which brings us right back to the beginning of the cycle—getting clear and setting an intention. Your reasons for pursuing a spiritual path, your own needs, the places where you want to grow, they are incredibly personal. Is it your intention to establish a regular spiritual practice, develop a creative community, or to bring things to completion more often?

Remember that the most useful intention is stated in terms of attitudes and actions, not specific outcomes. For example, you might consider an intention like "I am committed to completion" rather than "I complete everything I start." Similarly, "I actively nurture my creative community" might be a more open and active intention than something like "I am surrounded by a warm and nurturing creative community."

A Conversation with Commitment to Action

Consider what your intention might be. What is the attitude or action that you want to hold moving forward? Ask yourself...

- What is the role I want artmaking to have in my life?
- What is the role I want spiritual practice to have in my life?
- How do I most need to grow or change as a person?
- What needs does artmaking fill in my life?
- What needs does spiritual practice fill in my life?

The answers may hold clues to the intention that might serve you best. Next, consider what kind of regular practice or ritual would support that intention. Take some time to write out both your intention and 15–20 possible actions that might support it. Then, commit to at least one of those actions. The idea is to name what you are moving towards, and then commit to a set of actions that support your intention. Might you?...

- Get together with a group once a month to make art
- Commit to doing an artmaking project once a week
- Take five minutes every day to write a haiku
- Join a dance company
- Try a new recipe every weekend
- Go through this book again, this time doing different Artful Explorations than you did the first time
- Find another book on building or developing your creativity, and try reading it and doing the exercises in that book from the perspective of your intention
- Find another book on spirituality or spiritual practice, and try responding to each chapter or section of the book with an artmaking exploration of your own
- Replace one hour of passive entertainment each week with an hour of active creating

As you think about it, remember that your intentions may change or shift, and so might the kinds of things you need to do to support the intention. The practice is not set in stone; it grows and changes as you do. You may also need fallow times. Give yourself a way to take time off that makes sense to you and appeals to your needs for freedom or structure, while still maintaining a practice. Maybe you get one "goof-off" coupon a month, or you give yourself permission to let go of completion while you're on vacation. Maybe you commit to one artmaking retreat a month, and don't worry about the times in-between. This is a practice: You probably won't do it perfectly the first time, or even the second time. In fact, you'll probably never do it perfectly. You'll just keep practicing.

To exist is to change, to change is to mature, to mature is to go on creating oneself endlessly.

–Henri Bergson

Support and Accountability

We develop a creative community in part because it provides us both support and accountability as we work to develop and maintain a practice. Other community members can be there for us when it gets tough, as well as reminding us of why we choose to do this even when it feels like we don't want to. Part of the idea behind building a community of practice is that we surround ourselves with people living the kinds of lives we want to be living. We see people choosing to turn the TV off and spend time in the studio, or living more simply so that they have more time to write. We see people taking risks in their artmaking and surviving.

Creativity is a type of learning process where the teacher and pupil are located in the same individual.

–Arthur Koestler

Being in creative community means we are surrounded by examples of how to shift our own priorities and choices so that they support a creative and spiritual life. This is why something as simple as following a few inspiring people on Twitter and engaging them in conversations can help you to build and feel like part of a community—and why it can be a valuable support for your own practice.

These things also help to hold us accountable. There are other people cheering us on, wanting us to take that chance or try that new thing. They are not caught in the sticky web of our excuses. They are asking us, "Sorry your dog chewed up your favorite paint brush! How might you go about reaching completion on that painting anyway?" and they are emailing us metaphorical paintbrushes in support.

Accountability Adventures

Beyond simply cultivating community, we also need to actively do things to hold ourselves accountable, to help ourselves stick with our intentions and come to completion on the things we commit to. And sometimes we need to actively involve other people and ask them specifically to help us. We are real people in the real world, and the road to developing a practice is rough and lined with distractions. So, here are a few of my favorite Accountability Adventures, to use on your own or with a friend.

- Set aside time in your day planner or calendar for artmaking. This could be anything: a few minutes a day, a few hours a week, a few days a month. Don't let anything shift your schedule.
- When you commit to making art as a regular spiritual practice, write out a series of postcards to yourself. Use the postcards to record your intentions as you begin artmaking. Simple phrases like "I allow myself the same joy I had in artmaking as a child" or "I will approach artmaking as a way to explore" or "I am open to dialog with Spirit." Address and stamp the postcards. Mix them in with your bills and mail them to yourself, or give a stack to a friend to mail to you at regular intervals.
- Reward yourself with a trip to the art supply store each time you complete a piece.
- Sign up for a process-oriented artmaking class. Sometimes committing to someone else with your money is easier than committing to yourself.

Painting is an attempt to come to terms with life. There are as many solutions as there are human beings.

–George Tooker

Creativity means making something for the soul out of every experience.

–Thomas More

- Commit to teaching something you're learning. Agree to share one of the Artful Explorations with your niece with a "Come on over and do intuitive collage with me on Friday," or bring a friend along on an imagination walk. You'll find yourself forced to explain the ideas in your own words, and grappling with a friend's questions and challenges can help you clarify and strengthen your own understanding and commitment.
- Commit to doing some journaling or writing or discussion with a friend when you feel stuck or have a bout of resistance. It won't keep the resistance from happening, but it will make it easier to handle and easier to work through if you agree to seek some kind of support for it.
- Get involved in an online challenge or swap. If you do an online search for art blogs, art challenges, or art swaps (or visit one of the ones listed in the resources section of www.eyesaflame.com), you can discover a whole world of people trying new things and then either trading them or non-judgmentally posting images of their completed projects online. Many sites have challenges every week, so you can follow along for a few weeks to make sure you feel comfortable before jumping in. Or you can do the challenges on your own without sharing the results.
- Do the exercises in this book with a friend. Agree to meet on a regular basis.

Process, Practice, Pathway

I want to take a moment to remind you not to get too hung up on the order of the process, or how long each step takes, or doing it "right." Getting Clear, Getting Inspired, Getting Engaged, Staying in Touch, and Giving Back are simply ways of thinking about artmaking as playful prayer and breaking it down into manageable pieces. These pieces are containers for the components of the practice; they are stones paving the path. You may experience them as stepping stones leading you across a brook, or as a series of beautiful pebbles that reassuringly appear as you wander along a rocky beach. Do the steps in your own way. Make the process a practice that works for you.

Similarly, the individual bits of advice I offer for making the work of art easier—the attitudes and actions—are just that: advice. They are not hard and fast rules. Again, I encourage you to try them all:

Explore
Focus on Process, Not Product
Defer Judgment
Be Like a Novice
Be in Conversation
Be Mindful
Follow the Energy
Let Go of the Outcome
Be Curious
Tune Up Your Inner Ears
Cultivate Appreciation and Gratitude
Hold Clear Intentions

Apply those that work; let go the ones that don't. Which ones have come close to being habits? Which ones do you still struggle with?

Mandala

Mandala is a Sanskrit word meaning circle or whole. Visually, we recognize mandalas as images or collections of images that have been arranged with radial symmetry. They have a center, or focal point, around which other images radiate. We see this form frequently in nature, from the structure of flower petals around a stamen to the way our own limbs extend out from our heart to the way the planets orbit the sun. We are probably also familiar with images of mandalas from Buddhism, where these forms are sometimes described as mind support for use during meditation. Mandalas are used to describe an entire universe or tell a complete story, and are almost like spiritual maps.

Buddhism is not the only faith tradition that uses the mandala form. We see them in the round or "rose" stained glass windows in Christian churches and in the sand paintings of certain Native American tribes. And if we look at many of the forms that guide us and move us in secular life—the clock, the wheel, and the compass—it is not surprising that they also take a mandala form. The circle is the story of cycles, of movement, of the way that change is simply part of the natural order. The mandala gives a sense of focus, of direction, of place. It's perfect as a tool for intention.

Materials

- Square piece of heavy blank paper (larger is better)
- Pen or pencil
- Round items of different sizes (to be traced or used as guides)
- Ruler or straightedge
- Your favorite drawing, painting, or coloring materials

OPTIONAL

- Junk mail or old magazines
- Colored construction paper
- Scissors or craft knife
- Glue stick, Mod Podge, or gel medium
- Brushes and water container
- Wax paper or palette
- Acrylic paints and gesso
- Found objects and heavy craft glue

1. Consider your intention going forward. Take a few moments to journal about the intention, as well as any colors, symbols, textures, smells, phrases, animals, shapes, or other images that you associate with the intention.

3. Now, fill in the mandala with images, colors, shapes, textures, and objects that support the intention. You can use the ways you've divided up the space as guides or ideas for gluing in collaged images, obscuring the original lines.

4. You can fill in the entire mandala with hand-drawn patterns, or fill each space with flat color. You can combine collaged images, paint, or even three-dimensional objects. The choice is up to you. The intention is the outcome.

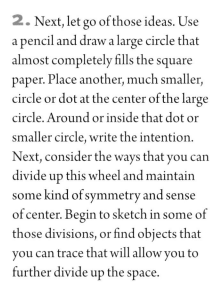

2. Next, let go of those ideas. Use a pencil and draw a large circle that almost completely fills the square paper. Place another, much smaller, circle or dot at the center of the large circle. Around or inside that dot or smaller circle, write the intention. Next, consider the ways that you can divide up this wheel and maintain some kind of symmetry and sense of center. Begin to sketch in some of those divisions, or find objects that you can trace that will allow you to further divide up the space.

TAKING IT FURTHER

Additional Materials
- Labyrinth
- Camera or camera phone

Consider mandalas in other forms. You may want to find a labyrinth in your city and walk it as a meditation. If labyrinths intrigue you as a possible moving meditation, you might be interested in the book *A Creative Walker's Guide to the Labyrinth: An Approach for Beginners* by Janice Francisco.

Or you may want to consider mandalas in nature. Go for a nature hike and search for natural occurrences of the mandala shape. You might even want to arrange natural objects in mandala forms à la artist Andy Goldsworthy. Try taking a camera with you, and photographing found and created mandalas.

Prayer Candle

Materials

- Blank Novena (a tall candle poured into a glass container or straight glass candleholder for a pillar candle)
- Junk mail or old magazines
- Other collage materials
- Pencil or pen
- Glue stick
- Scissors or craft knife
- Mod Podge or gel medium
- Tape measure or ruler
- Blank paper or sketchbook
- Access to a scanner/printer or color photocopier

OPTIONAL

- Colorful tissue paper
- Hot glue gun or heavy craft glue
- Lightweight found objects (like buttons, beads, glitter, and feathers)

1. Consider your intention for your creative practice. What images, colors, symbols, or figures represent that intention? There might be an image of the Divine, such as the Virgin of Guadalupe or Quan Yin, who embodies some attitude you wish to hold. Or there might be a symbol, object, or animal that embodies an attitude or action you aspire to.

2. Next, gather your images and collage materials. Because you are going to be backlighting this image, I recommend making your collage and then photocopying it rather than adhering your collage elements directly to the candleholder's surface from the start. This way, the image glows, rather than the light simply revealing what's on the reverse side of the paper or the many layers that have been glued on the surface.

3. Consider the dimensions of your novena or glass candleholder. How big does the collage copy need to be to wrap around the glass and meet in the back? Or do you want to create an image that will be a medallion, a focal image visible from the front only? Use a tape measure or ruler to determine the size. Remember that you can shrink or enlarge the photocopy if needed. Now, begin your collage.

4. When you're done, photocopy your image onto regular copy paper (or scan and print using smudge-proof inks). You don't want the paper to be so heavy that light won't shine through it.

5. Next, trim the image as needed and get ready to adhere it to your novena candle or glass candle holder. You can apply the Mod Podge to the paper or directly on the glass; you can apply the adhesive all at once, or in sections as you roll the paper on. Either way, line up one edge of the paper on the glass, and begin smoothing the paper onto the surface, being careful to eliminate air bubbles.

6. Add embellishments like beads, buttons, or feathers. For non-paper embellishments, use either a hot glue gun or a heavy craft glue like Tacky Glue or Ultimate Craft Glue to adhere them to the surface. The candle won't get hot enough to melt the hot glue. Areas of the glass that aren't filled with your collage image can be covered with layers of colored tissue paper. Light shines through the tissue paper like stained glass when it's been applied in layers with Mod Podge or gel medium.

7. If you need some bling, glitter can be applied to the surface in a glitter glue form, or in a powdered form using a lighter glue like Elmer's or even Mod Podge. Make sure that the flame of the candle won't be coming in contact with any of the embellishments. This is why we decorate candleholders and novena candles in glass rather than the pillar candles themselves—less fire risk!

TAKING IT FURTHER

Additional Materials

- Scanner/Printer
- Shrinkable plastic (the kind that can be run through your home printer)
- Parchment paper
- Oven
- Blank nightlight kit
- Goop or E6000

OPTIONAL

- Beads
- Wire (22 gauge)
- ⅛" hole punch

A favorite adaptation of this in my classes is the Guardian Nightlight. Here, you take your collage (you can even use your collage of the Ally from Chapter 9) and print it onto shrink plastic for use in a nightlight!

1. Scan your image and get it the right size. Usually, an image that measures between 5" × 7" and 7.5" × 10" before shrinking will result in a nice size for a night light. Follow the directions on the package of shrink plastic to print the image. Be careful to reduce the amount of ink you use—because the plastic shrinks, you'll need less ink than usual to get bright color in the final product.

2. Next, trim any sharp corners. These will be very sharp once it bakes! If you want to use wire to add beads or other adornments to the nightlight, punch ⅛" holes in the plastic before you shrink it. The plastic is very hard to cut once it's shrunk.

3. Follow the package instructions to shrink the plastic. Try placing your piece of printed shrink plastic in a little folded envelope made of parchment paper and close it with staples or metal brads before baking. This will help keep the plastic from curling over on itself during the shrinking.

4. Use oven mitts and remove the shrunken plastic. Quickly flatten out any remaining unevenness while it's still warm. Once it cools, use wire to attach beads to the surface. Finally, use Goop or E6000 to attach the shrink plastic to the nightlight blank.

More detailed instructions for this nightlight project, resources for materials, and instructions for other fun projects can be found on my website, www.eyesaflame.com.

A Big Hug until Next Time

Making art allows me to listen, it allows me to speak, and it allows me to pray. It allows me to connect and communicate with my inner self, Spirit, and my greater community. If I go more than a week or so without making art of some kind, I start to get cranky, restless, even depressed. Artmaking as playful prayer has brought me to a more connected, energized, and grounded place in my life.

Not everyone who reads this book or tries making art on a regular basis in the ways I suggest will experience the same result. However, if what you read and try here helps you find a way to make art a little more often, a little more joyfully, a little more meaningfully, and with a greater sense of connection, then I will consider it a success.

In the meantime, I am still practicing. I hope you are, too.

Thank you.

Bibliography and Resources

References and Books in Print

The following are great books on the creative process, spirituality, devotional and spiritual artmaking, and lifelong learning. They are also the books I referred to when writing this book.

Allen, P. B. (1995). *Art is a way of knowing*. Boston: Shambhala.

Allen, P. B. (2005). *Art is a spiritual path*. Boston: Shambhala.

Arettam, J. (2001). *Spirit maps: Follow the exquisite geometry of art and nature back to your center*. Boston: Red Wheel/Weiser.

Ayto, J. (1990). *Dictionary of word origins: The histories of more than 8,000 English-language words*. New York: Arcade Publishing.

Azara, N. (2002). *Spirit taking form: Making a spiritual practice of making art*. Boston: Red Wheel.

Barber, V. (2002). *Explore yourself through art*. New York: Plume/Penguin Putnam.

Booth, E. (1999). *The everyday work of art*. Naperville, IL: Sourcebooks.

Cameron, J., & Bryan, M. (1992). *The artist's way: A spiritual path to higher creativity*. New York: G. P. Putnam.

Cano-Murillo, K. (2002). *Making shadow boxes and shrines*. Glouchester, MA: Rockport.

Cassou, M., & Cubley, S. (1995). *Life, paint and passion: Reclaiming the magic of spontaneous expression*. New York: Jeremy P. Tarcher/Putnam.

Crockett, T. (2000). *The artist inside: A spiritual guide to cultivating your creative self*. New York: Broadway Books.

Cunningham, B. (2002). *Mandala: Journey to the center*. New York: Dorling Kindersley.

Csikszentmihalyi, M. (1990). *Flow: The psychology of optimal experience*. New York: HarperCollins.

Francisco, J. (2006). *A creative walker's guide to the labyrinth: An approach for beginners*. Ottowa: BridgePoint Effect.

Frost, S. (2001). *SoulCollage: An intuitive collage process for individuals and groups*. Santa Cruz, CA: Hanford Mead.

Goldsworthy, A. (1990). *A collaboration with nature*. New York: Harry N. Abrams.

Hellmuth, C. (2003). *Collage discovery workshop*. Cincinnati, OH: North Light Books.

Kingston, K. (1999). *Clear your clutter with feng shui*. New York: Broadway Books.

Koff-Chapin, D. (1996). *Drawing out your soul: The touch drawing handbook*. Langley, WA: The Center for Touch Drawing.

Lundy, R. (2003). *Crafts for the spirit: 30 beautiful projects to enhance your personal journey*. New York: Lark Books.

Maisel, E. (2011). *Mastering creative anxiety: 24 lessons for writers, painters, musicians and actors from America's foremost creativity coach*. Novato, CA: New World Library. Quote reprinted with permission.

Mandali, M. (2004). *Everyone's mandala coloring book* (13th printing). Helena, MT: Author.

MacKenzie, G. (1996). *Orbiting the giant hairball: A corporate fool's guide to surviving with grace*. New York: Viking.

McMann, J. (1998). *Altars and icons: Sacred spaces in everyday life*. San Francisco: Chronicle Books.

Miller, B., Vehar, J., & Firestien, R., (2001). *Creativity unbound: An introduction to creative process*. New York: Innovation Resources.

Nimmer, D. (2008). Art from intuition: Overcoming your fears and obstacles to making art. New York: Watson-Guptill.

Puccio, G. J., Murdock, M. C., & Mance, M., (2007). *Creative leadership: Skills that drive change*. Thousand Oaks, CA: Sage.

Vaill, P. B. (1996). *Learning as a way of being: Strategies for survival in a world of permanent white water*. San Francisco: Jossey-Bass.

Vaill, P. B. (1998). *Spirited leading and learning: Process wisdom for a new age*. San Francisco: Jossey-Bass.

Waldman, D. (2002). *Joseph Cornell: Master of dreams*. New York: Harry N. Abrams.

Wall, C. L. (2004). *The courage to trust: A guide to building deep and lasting relationships*. Oakland, CA: New Harbinger.

Webster's New Twentieth Century Dictionary: Unabridged (2nd ed.) (1979). USA: William Collins.

Whyte, D. (2002). *Clear mind, wild heart* [CD]. Louisville, CO: Sounds True.

Wiley, S., & Shannon, M. O. (2002). A string and a prayer: How to make and use prayer beads. San Francisco: Red Wheel.

Wise, N. (2002). *A big new free happy unusual life: Self-expression and spiritual practice for those who have time for neither*. New York: Broadway Books.

Zander, R. S., & Zander, B. (2000). *The art of possibility*. Boston: Harvard Business School Press.

Materials and Resources

RUBBER STAMPS http://www.fredbmullett.com For amazing nature print stamps by Fred Mullett that appear in collages throughout this book. These stamps and images were used in this book with permission from Fred B. Mullett.

ACRYLIC PAINTS http://www.goldenpaints.com Wonderful acrylic paints and mediums, and a very useful artist help line.

TAROT CARDS http://www.osho.com You can order your own set of the Osho Zen Tarot (with amazing images by Deva Padma) directly from Osho International Foundation or from Amazon. Images from the Osho Zen Tarot appear with permission from Osho International Foundation.

Online: Workshops and Reference

Process Painting, Touch Drawing, and SoulCollage are all specific techniques that embody process-oriented approaches to artmaking, and I highly recommend workshops with any of these instructors or those who have been trained in their techniques. These terms, along with phrases like "expressive arts," can be entered into your search engine to help you find art classes and workshops that veer away from a focus on product or "perfect outcomes."

http://www.processarts.com (information on workshops with Stewart Cubley)

http://www.touchdrawing.com (a technique developed by Deborah Koff-Chapin)

http://www.soulcollage.com (a technique developed by Seena Frost)

http://www.eyesaflame.com (a listing of my own upcoming workshops and events, as well as a variety of free project ideas and tutorials)

Appendix A
A Note on Theory and Practice

In 2003, when I was trying to figure out what kind of work I wanted to do that incorporated creativity and spirituality, I made a list of all the times during my work —paid and unpaid— that I had experienced flow. I was trying to identify those moments when, as David Whyte put it, I felt like I had "brought the whole person to work." Turns out, I had felt it during a huge variety of tasks, from sorting questionnaire responses to painting. I had felt it while planning events, designing marketing strategies, and even editing reports.

Before long, I had a list of 40 or 50 different activities that had allowed me to experience flow, even if briefly. I grouped these tasks loosely into categories, and then realized they represented a cycle of inter-related activities. As I developed the ideas in the cycle, I came to realize that it described not only how I wanted to work, it also described how I wanted to make art and how I wanted to live my life—with clarity, inspiration, engagement, and giving, while staying firmly in touch with my values and listening to the voice of intuition. These became what I thought of as my Factors for Creative Flow, and as it developed into a practice, it also became the basis for Artmaking as Playful Prayer.

Not long after, I began studying Creativity and Change Leadership at the International Center for Studies in Creativity in Buffalo, New York. It was then that I began to see parallels between my own personal idea and other, more thoroughly researched theories. The cycle I had identified bore a strong similarity to the Creative Problem Solving Process, or CPS, initially identified by ad executive Alex Osborn in the early 1950s and further refined by Osborn and education researcher Dr. Sidney Parnes in the 1960s. While various scholars and practitioners have made adjustments to Osborn and Parnes' model and others continue to refine it, CPS remains the basis for much of our current understanding of applied creativity or creative process.

In its most basic form, Creative Problem Solving can be reduced to these four main steps:
- Finding, understanding, and clarifying the problem
- Generating ideas
- Selecting, developing, and refining the solution
- Gaining acceptance for and implementing the solution

It sounds a lot like Get Clear, Get Inspired, Get Engaged, and Give Back! A more recent description of the process in the 2007 book *Creative Leadership: Skills That Drive Change* by PhDs Gerard Puccio, Mary Murdock, and Marie Mance includes a step for ongoing assessment. This step is placed in the center of the chart describing the process—which is remarkably similar to my concept of Staying in Touch.

The theory of CPS has developed, in part, through observing highly productive creative professionals and the processes they use as they work. Osborn ran an ad agency, and he developed the process as a way of utilizing the valuable input of both the creative team and the business team. He emphasized using both divergent and convergent thinking styles in all phases of the process because it worked in the real world. Osborn and Parnes believed that creativity, as a skill, could be developed, and that CPS could be used to find workable solutions for any vague and poorly defined problem without a set answer. Osborn set about establishing the Creative Education Foundation with the goal of teaching everyone how to solve complex problems from "How might we make this relationship work?" to "How might I fill the blank canvas?"

Viewed this way, creative problem solving—and understanding how creativity works—is an essential life skill. It is relevant outside of creative professions like architecture and advertising where it was originally studied. It is useful for all areas of business and entrepreneurship. It is applicable in education. And yes, even artists and spiritual seekers may find it of interest.

As I continued to study and develop my own flow-and-spirituality-based cycle of creativity, I also found that there were parallels between my five factors and the elements of the whole person discussed by educators and business leaders from Stephen Covey to David Whyte. When I read Pat B. Allen's *Art Is a Spiritual Path*, I also saw a strong overlap between my playful prayer cycle and the process she guides her students through at the Art Institute of Chicago.

I am convinced that the similarity I see between my approach and the approach of other creative professionals, creativity researchers, educators, and leaders is because this idea of a cycle of both spiritual and creative flow is something that resonates strongly with us as human beings. We keep seeing it and trying to name it because it's actually already a natural part of us.

Appendix B
A Note on Working with Groups

I took my first job teaching art when I was 20. Now, with my 40 in the rear view mirror, I can see how much I've learned since that first batik class, and how much I still have to learn about groups and how to work with them. During the process of teaching and working on this book, the honest feedback of my colleagues and students has taught me a great deal. Most significantly, I have come to realize the importance of witnessing and celebration in a group setting. I now do more planning before my sessions and gather more feedback after, and I am working to include more formalized times for check-ins. Even with a Master's degree that focused largely on how to facilitate creativity in groups, there's still a lot I don't know.

I designed this book so that it could serve as an individual workshop-in-a-book, and I'm sure some of you will want to share the contents of this book with friends. I chose not to include information on facilitating ArtMaking as Playful Prayer groups in this book for several reasons. First, trying to include group explorations proved distracting to the individual focus of the book, and second, I wanted more time to test and refine the group activities.

That said, I encourage you to meet with friends and make art together using the Artful Explorations in this book! I am already pulling notes together for a Group Facilitator's Guide. In the meantime, if you feel called to facilitate a group program from this book, and charge people to participate, I simply ask three things as a courtesy: First, please read the book start to finish, and try any projects and Artful Explorations on your own before asking the group to do them (this can help with troubleshooting!). Second, please credit me and the book in any workshop promotion you do. Third, purchase a copy of the book for each participant as part of the workshop and include that cost as part of the fee you charge. If you do end up facilitating or participating in a group, I'd love to hear about your experiences!

Index

E

elements 38, 69
energy 10, 21, 24–25, 28, 68, 78, 87–97, 102, 115–116, 129, 132
engage 67–69, 75, 77–79, 99–104, 115, 153
exploration 13–15, 22, 29, 51, 68, 87, 89–90, 133, 168
explore **15**, 16–19, 68

F

faith 9, 15, 38, 141, 153
fallow 118, 154
flow 21, **67**, 68–69, 75, 79, 87, 99, 129, 167–168
flow factors 13, 67–69, 127, 141, 156
focus on process, not product 11, 28, 30–33
follow the energy 93, 94–97, 102, 115, 129, 132

G–H

getting clear 13, 68, 75–79, 127, 141, 156
getting engaged 13, 68, 99–104, 127, 141, 156
getting inspired 13, 68, 87–93, 127, 141, 156
giving back 13, 68, 127, 141–145, 156
glue (see also adhesives) 41–43, 51–52, 55–56
goofing off 91, 118
gratitude 91, 142–143, 146–151
hold clear intentions 75–79, 153–154, 157–163

I

idea 26, 88, 92–93
inner ears 102, 127, 129, 134–139
inner voice 11, 49, 103, 127–128, 133
inspiration 68–69, **87**–93, 118
inspiration (myths of) 87
intention 22, 68, **75**–79, 87, 101–102, 153–154, 157–163
intuition 68, 101–103, **127**–133

J–K

journal 14, 37, 49, 52, 93, 102, 118, 132–133
judgment 29, **40**, 41–48, 49, 113–114, 128
Kingston, Karen 79

L

learning 15, 25, 39, 91, 133, 155
let go of the outcome 101–102, 104, 105–111, 143
letting go (of the story) 102–103
like 104, 143
listening 21, 25, 39, 102, 127, 132

M

materials 51–59, 60
Mckenzie, Gordon 23
meaning 10, 15, 22–23, 26, **115**
meaningful 11, 22–23, 67, **115**
mindfulness **76**–77, 79
mindful 22, 29, 67–68, 76–78, 80–85

N–O

notes 15, 26, 28, 53, 58, 69, 104
novice **39**
online 141–142, 156, 166
Osborn, Alex 69, 167

P

packrat 58–59
painting 37, 44–48, 52–58, 67, 79, 94–96, 103, 105–108, 115, 117, 128, 156
painting experience 40, 166
Parnes, Sidney 69, 167
perfection 28, 40, 60, 68, 90–92, 129
play 25, 27, 40, 60, 68, 90–92, 129
playful **25**, 90–92
practice 9–11, 14, 37, 39, 68–69, 87–88, 99, 145, 153–156, 167
prayer 24–**25**, 67, 75, 115, 127, 148–151
precious 59
process painting 10, 55, 166

process (of artmaking) 39–40, 67–69
    (of flow) (see also creativity and creative problem solving) 67–69
    (of creativity) (see creativity and creative problem solving)
process vs. product 28–29
product 11, 21–22, 28, 75, 88, 117
professional 15, 24, 28

R

relationship 10, 25
religion 24
resistance 67, 91, 100–101, 113–118, 156
resolve 99
risk 28, 101, 104, 116
ritual 9, 153–154

S

sacred **37**, 35–40
self-expression 67, 115, 132
sharing 11, 78, 100, 132, **142**, 141–145
Shaw, Robert 24
shrine (see also altar) 58–59, 71–72, 115
solve vs. resolve 99–100
spirit 10, 21, 24–25, 67, 87–88, 127, 132–133, 143
spiritual connection 37, 67–68, 129–130, 133
spiritual practice 9–10, 14, 21–25, 37–39, 87–88, 99, 145, 153–155
spirituality 9–10, 21, **24**, 69, 167
staying in touch 10, 13, 68, 127–133, 156, 167
studio 28, 35–38, 58–59, 79, 155
support 13–14, 37, 39, 76, 130, 142, 154–155

T–Z

teaching 10–11, 21, 23, 38, 145, 168
tune up your inner ears 102, 127, 129, 134–139
value 130–132, 134–136
will and surrender ,dance of 25, 76, 99, 132
work of art 22–23, 68, 79, 87, 89, 133, 156